WITHDRAWN BY THE
UNIVERSITY OF MICHIGAN

THE CRISIS IN WELFARE IN CLEVELAND

Cleveland. Commission on

THE CRISIS IN WELFARE IN CLEVELAND

REPORT OF THE MAYOR'S COMMISSION

EDITED BY HERMAN D. STEIN
Chairman

CASE WESTERN RESERVE UNIVERSITY
CLEVELAND / 1969

HV
87
.C6
A45

Acknowledgment is gratefully made to the individuals and groups who contributed funds to subsidize the publication of this report.

Copyright © 1969 by Case Western Reserve University, Cleveland, Ohio 44106.

All rights reserved.

Printed in the United States of America.

Standard Book Number: 8295-0160-6 (cloth).
8295-0164-9 (paper).

Library of Congress Catalogue Card Number: 69-17687.

FOREWORD

At the beginning of the winter season 1967–68 it became painfully evident that there were thousands of Cleveland children who would not have adequate clothing to shield them from the cold and that those who were forced to live on welfare were in desperate need. Newly elected Mayor Carl B. Stokes gave two assurances: first, that the proceeds of his Inaugural Ball would go for the purposes of clothing the children and, second, that he would find out why, in a prosperous state and county, tens of thousands of children are inadequately fed and clothed. He kept his first promise—although the proceeds could hardly meet the major needs—and, to carry out the second, he appointed a Commission on the Crisis in Welfare and asked that it submit a report in June 1968.

His letter[1] inviting Dr. Herman D. Stein to be Chairman, said, in part:

> As Mayor of the City of Cleveland, I now hope to take steps which will be helpful in solving this critical and tragic inadequacy. It is my intention to create a Commission on the Crisis in Welfare, to be composed of representatives of private and public leadership in Cleveland, the religious community which has been active towards solving the problem, and members of the poverty community itself. I am charging this Commission to determine just what the situation of the needy children is, how it got that way, and what should be done about it. Moreover, I am requesting the Commission to examine the relationship of government to this situation at municipal, county, state and Federal levels. I am asking that the relationship of business, labor, the professions and the public at large be studied in detail.

The chairman and members of the Commission were appointed in early January, 1968. The modest budget was pre-

---

[1]Reproduced in Appendix A.

pared with the expectation, since realized, that the three major faiths would support this activity. Space and furnishings for the Commission's work were provided by Case Western Reserve University. A small staff was engaged, and the membership of the Commission was organized for its work. The volunteer services of experts, citizens, students, and others who expressed a wish to cooperate were promptly put to work. The Commission had its first meeting within two weeks after the Mayor announced its creation. Five work groups were developed, which met weekly: One dealt with the problem of finances and relations between city, county, and state, and between the private and public sectors. A second studied the administrative practices and policies within the welfare operation itself. A third was concerned with the rights of welfare clientele and with major problems of welfare clients related to health care, schooling, and housing. A fourth work group concentrated on the areas of employment and training, and a fifth on issues of public information.

Two principles have been important to the Commission's work. First, it would use all existing facts and studies wherever possible, rather than launch any large scale research of its own. Such studies include those of the Ohio Civil Rights Commission, the Inner-City Action Committee, the Welfare Federation of Cleveland, and the County Welfare Department itself. Second, if there were public positions the Commission should take on matters it could help correct during the course of its work, such positions should be taken even though fact-gathering and analysis were still in progress. Two such positions have been taken by the Commission, one on the county health and welfare levy, since approved by the voters, and the other on the release of state funds earmarked for needy children. The Governor and Legislature of Ohio did not accomplish the latter, despite the efforts of Mayor Stokes, Senators Robert Taft, Jr., and M. Morris Jackson, the Welfare Federation, the Commission, and other interested citizens.

Several of the recommendations of working groups and the Commission itself have been implemented or given expression by others, either as a matter of coincidence or familiarity with the Commission's thinking. Thus, the announcement of the Cuyahoga County Commissioners' proposal to seek an increase in the levy from 2 to 3 mills took place the day after a Commission work group recommended it; a reorganization of the

County Welfare Advisory Board was announced after the Commission had discussed and acted on the recommendation; Mayor Stokes' recommendations made at the recent U.S. Conference of Mayors for a national minimum income for those unable to work and for guaranteed jobs for the employable were also made public, as were his statements on health care. If the Commission's efforts were related to these and similar developments, its members consider it all to the good. If they were unrelated, the Commission is gratified by the similarity and reinforcement of positions.

This report is not "balanced" in its consideration of institutions in Cuyahoga County, in the sense of assessing the pros and cons of these institutions. The accent is on problems and unmet or insufficiently met needs. The tone of the report in these sections is therefore critical, with little reference to positive accomplishments. We realize that there is excellent work done by many agencies and that there exist devoted, intelligent leadership and staff competence in both the public and private sectors. Our mission, however, was to concentrate on the problems of the poor, particularly those on welfare, to help determine why "the crisis" exists and what to do about it. It is this mission which required our focusing on shortcomings, and not any lack of respect of Commission members for the leadership, competence, or dedication of many citizens of Greater Cleveland, nor any lack of appreciation for the many constructive actions that have been taken in our community.

ACKNOWLEDGMENTS

The work of the Commission on the Crisis in Welfare has been made possible by the financial support of the three major faiths of Cleveland; the Catholic Diocese of Cleveland, the Jewish Community Federation of Cleveland, and the Council of Churches of Greater Cleveland shared the cost of the task assigned the Commission by Mayor Carl B. Stokes. Their participation as financial sponsors of this effort is testimony to the high concern and priority which the religious community places on the Crisis in Welfare.

This report is based on the efforts of scores of people—Commission members and staff, resource persons, and consultants—and has no single authorship. It represents the distillation not only of many hundreds of pages of minutes and documents but primarily the deliberations of the Commission over a six-month period. Most of its members devoted many hours every week to work group meetings, field visits, Commission meetings, and the study and preparation of materials. Great appreciation is due to Sidney Spector and George Livingston and to the secretarial staff, who gave unstintingly of their time and energy, without regard to the limits of a normal workday, to keep the work of the Commission going through myriad tasks and severe time pressure.

The Commission is grateful to Case Western Reserve University for providing without charge the three rooms in University House that housed the Commission's offices. The Commission is also appreciative of the meeting space provided its many committees and plenary sessions by churches and civic organizations. In addition, the staff in my own office in the university were of immense help, particularly during the final weeks, when this report was being organized and edited.

Finally, in submitting this Report to the Mayor the Commission extends its appreciation to the many professional consultants and resource specialists, to the volunteer assistants, and to the city officials, agency heads, and their staffs who cooperated in providing invaluable information and data without which the Commission's work would have been impossible. Their names are appended.

June 25, 1968

HERMAN D. STEIN
Chairman

COMMISSION MEMBERS

Dr. Herman D. Stein, Chairman
Colonel Giles C. Barrett
Mr. Fred Benbow
Mr. Ralph Besse
Miss Leona Bevis
Mrs. Verna Blunt
Dr. Douglas Bond‡
Rev. Milan C. Brenkus
Rev. DeForrest Brown‡
Rt. Rev. John H. Burt†
Mr. Hugh Calkins
Rev. Edward J. Camille†
Rev. E. T. Caviness†
Dr. K. Laurence Chang
Mrs. Marie Childress

Very Rev. Msgr. Casimir Ciolek
Mr. W. Rex Davis
Mr. Harry Derricott
Most Rt. Rev. Clarence E. Elwell
Mrs. Louise Gaston
Mr. William Ginn†
Mr. Wilbur Grattan, Sr.
Mr. Burt W. Griffin
Dr. Nathan Grundstein
Rev. Donald G. Jacobs
Mr. Sam Janis‡
Mrs. Lee Jordan
Mr. Irving Kane‡
Mr. Richard Kelley‡
Mrs. Carole King

Mr. Mitchell Kress
Mr. David Leahy
Mr. Sebastian Lupica
Dr. Charles McClelland
Dr. James G. Miller
Mr. Roy B. Miner
Mr. Steven A. Minter
Dr. James A. Norton
Rev. Charles W. Rawlings
Dr. Willard C. Richan
Dr. Marvin Rosenberg

Mr. Maurice B. Saltzman
Mrs. Alberta Sawyer
Mr. Harry T. Sealy
Rabbi Daniel J. Silver†
Mr. Arthur B. Tillman
Mr. Charles Tricarichi
Mr. James J. Urban
Mr. Sidney Vincent
Rev. B. Bruce Whittemore
Mrs. Helen Williams
Mr. Kay Williams

COMMISSION STAFF

Mr. Sidney Spector—Director*
Mr. George Livingston—Assistant Director; Acting Director*
Mrs. Samuel Brown—Administrative Assistant
Mrs. Juanita Jones—Secretary
Mrs. Doris J. Long—Secretary
Mrs. Gwendolyn Noles—Secretary

Dr. Stein's Office Staff

Mrs. Helen DuBov
Mrs. Ralph E. Wightman

VOLUNTEER STAFF ASSISTANTS

Miss Barbara Ashley
Mr. Terrence Bartlett
Mr. Kevin Donnelly
Miss Joanne Hall
Mr. Arthur Lifson
Mr. Michael Mascari

Miss Susan Plock
Mr. Steven Shanklin
Mr. Lawrence Siegel
Mrs. Marian Stewart
Mr. Gale Ward

RESOURCE AND CONSULTATION

Mr. Paul Abels
Mr. John Adams
Mr. Kwegyir Aggrey
Mr. Sidney Andorn
Mrs. Mildred Barry
Mr. Roldo Bartimole
Mr. Howard Berger
Dr. Arthur Blum
Mr. Robert Bond

Mr. Ralph Brody
Mr. Robert Carr
Mr. Daniel T. Carroll
Mr. Jay Chunn
Dr. Frank Cliffe, Jr.
Mr. Ernest Cooper
Mrs. Erlynne Davis
Dr. Jane DeMelto (Deceased)
Mr. Andrew Dobelstein

---

*Mr. Spector resigned as Staff Director on April 19, 1968, upon being assigned responsibilities in the city administration by Mayor Stokes. At that time, Mr. Livingston became Acting Director.

†Chairman of a special working group.

‡Vice-Chairman of a special working group.

Mrs. Lois Dupree
Mr. Melvin Durschlag
Dr. Harold Enarson
Mr. Myron W. Goldman
Mr. Troy Grigsby
Mr. Murray Gruber
Mr. Peter Halbin
Mr. Robert Handleman
Mr. Clarence Holmes
Mrs. Joanne Kaufman
Mr. Sidney Lewine
Mrs. Archie Lewis
Mr. W. T. McCullough
Mr. Bernard Olshansky
Mr. Richard Overmyer
Mrs. Helen Randall
Mr. Sol Rosenbaum
Mr. George Sapin
Mr. Estal Sparlin
Mr. Michael Stanton
Rev. Donald Stockford
Mr. Robert Taber
Mr. Gregory Taylor
Dr. Donald Thomas
Mrs. Marymal Williams
Dr. Robert Williams
Dr. Ellen Winston

Staff Members of: Social and Rehabilitation Service and Office of Education, U.S. Department of Health, Education, and Welfare, Washington, D.C.

AGENCY OFFICIALS AND STAFF MEMBERS INTERVIEWED BY THE COMMISSION

CUYAHOGA COUNTY WELFARE DEPARTMENT

Mr. Eugene Burns, Director
Mrs. Roberta Allport
Mr. Torild Barbins
Mr. Robert Casey
Mrs. Dahl J. Davis
Mr. Earl Davis
Mr. James Easterling
Mrs. Jean Giebink
Mrs. Alvira Goffney
Mr. Joseph Novak
Mrs. Margaret Rogers
Mrs. Ruth Saunders
Mr. John Small
Mrs. Leila Smith
Mrs. Magdalena Thomas
Miss Elisabeth Tuttle
Mr. Thomas D. Weiler

COUNCIL FOR ECONOMIC OPPORTUNITY

Mr. Ralph W. Findley, Director
Mrs. Madeline Cargill
Outreach Workers and Supervisors
Mr. Frank Catliota
Mr. Curtis Hall

UNIVERSITY HOSPITALS

Mr. Stanley Ferguson

CLEVELAND BOARD OF EDUCATION

Dr. Paul W. Briggs, Superintendent
Dr. Joseph L. Mazur
Dr. George Theobald

CUYAHOGA COUNTY COMMISSIONERS

Mr. William P. Day
Mr. Frank Gorman
Mr. Frank Pokorny

COUNTY ADMINISTRATOR

Mr. Lawrence Murtaugh

PREFACE

RESPONSE BY MAYOR CARL B. STOKES TO THE REPORT OF THE MAYOR'S COMMISSION ON THE CRISIS IN WELFARE

Last January I appointed a commission to examine the crisis in welfare in this community. In my letter to Dr. Herman Stein, inviting him to be chairman, I charged the Commission to determine just how serious the situation of needy children is, how it got that way, and what should be done about it.

I am pleased to state that this commission has fulfilled its charge. The report is a comprehensive analysis of the problem. It examines every significant aspect of economic dependency and makes recommendations to every sector of our community.

The Commission not only fulfilled its obligation to analyze how and why this situation developed, but, of greater importance, it set forth a detailed plan of action addressed to all levels of government, the business community, the voluntary sector, and the general public. I am convinced that if we are not able, as a community and a nation, to move in the direction of these recommendations, the problems will become even more explosive and will seriously threaten the stability of our society.

FEDERAL LEVEL RECOMMENDATIONS

An Adequate Income. First and foremost, the Commission recommended a national program of income supplements which will assure every unemployable individual in this nation an income at least equal to the federally determined poverty level.

Guaranteed Employment. Coupled with this recommendation, the Commission called for a policy of guaranteed full employment for all those able to work. Such a policy would encourage the private sector to expand employment to full capacity, with the federal government financing the special costs of the program, through private industry and through local government, as the employer of last resort.

As you know, I have already committed myself to both the income supplement and full employment propositions. I gave testimony to this effect to the National Platform Committee of the Democratic Party. In addition, Mayor Lindsay of New York City and I made these same recommendations to the U.S. Conference of Mayors. These recommendations were adopted by the Conference and a special committee of mayors was appointed to advance the recommendations in the White House and the Congress. *As a member of that committee, I intend to press for enactment of these recommendations now.*

1967 Social Security Amendments. I fully support the recommendation of the Commission in its call for the repeal of the freeze on dependent children under the AFDC program. This provision of the 1967 Social Security Amendments is a deliberately punitive attack on the poor. The Congress should also remove those provisions which discriminate against mothers who wish to care for their dependent children.

These provisions only serve to perpetuate the myth that employable mothers on public assistance prefer welfare payments to employment. All evidence points to the contrary. Most mothers on the welfare rolls—even those who are unemployable—would prefer earned income.

The fact of the matter is that we have not been able to provide decent paying jobs for even a fraction of these women seeking employment. In many cases the income from service occupations is so low that the mother is shortchanging her family by taking these jobs.

Day Care. In addition, those who laud the mandatory work provision must be reminded that the program is based on the assumption that day care will be provided for working mothers. Until now Ohio has chosen not to participate in the federal program for which the federal government would provide 85% matching funds if the state has an acceptable state-wide day care plan.

Today, eleven day care centers, operated by the County Welfare Department for working mothers, are in jeopardy of being discontinued because of the state's indifference. The responsibility for this deficiency clearly rests with the State Department of Public Welfare and the Governor.

I intend to press the State Department of Public Welfare to develop a suitable day care plan that will enable us to vastly expand our day care programs for low-income families.

STATE LEVEL RECOMMENDATIONS

The Commission made additional recommendations for action at the state level.

State Welfare Payments. The most important of these concerns the intolerably low standard of welfare payments paid by the state. The report discloses that payments in our city do not even meet the minimum standards of health and decency set by the state itself. *In addition, I agree with the Commission that the state standards are completely unrealistic to meet today's needs.*

I intend to use the full influence of my office to have the state's standards raised at least to the poverty level as determined by the federal government. This was recommended by the Commission.

State Welfare Funds. Presently $8.5 million in appropriated welfare funds are not being used for their earmarked purpose. I am very disturbed by the fact that the Governor and the General Assembly have allowed funds that were specially designated for increasing the level of payments to be used for other purposes.

We are again facing the prospect of seeing young children on welfare trudging to school through the winter snow with torn tennis shoes. Why must children suffer such deprivation when $8.5 million designated for this purpose are presently available? *The state can relieve this misery by releasing this money immediately to raise payments to minimum standards.*

This past spring our community demonstrated its concern for welfare recipients by enacting an increase in the health and welfare levy. This expression of concern and responsibility at the municipal level must be reciprocated at the state level, as implied in the 1964 reorganization of the welfare system. The state restricted the county's taxing authority and took upon itself the major responsibility for the administration of welfare programs.

A State Income Tax. To increase welfare payments to at least the poverty line level will require additional taxes. *The Commission spelled this out clearly and recommended a position to which I can subscribe and to which all responsible citizens should subscribe.*

There can be no equivocating with the fact that the only substantial and equitable source of revenue is through a state income tax. More than 30 states have come to this same conclusion after exhaustive analysis of the issues.

Such a broadly based, equitable tax on personal and corporate income would provide revenue not only for improved welfare payments but for improved education and health programs that will prevent future generations from becoming dependent on public assistance.

I support a state income tax and will call for the enactment of appropriate legislation at the next session of the Ohio General Assembly. Such legislation must ensure that cities in Ohio will receive adequate tax revenues from the income tax, either shared or independently levied, to cope more effectively with their urban problems. In this manner the state will assume its rightful responsibility and permit reductions in our heavily overloaded local property tax.

Title XIX. Another important recommendation of the Commission relates to the provision of medical services to low-income people in this community.

There are many working families not eligible for welfare payments but in desperate straits because of sudden overwhelming medical expenses. There is a special provision in the Medicaid bill for such medically indigent families, but Ohio does not participate in this program.

The people of Cleveland are losing out on hundreds of thousands of federal dollars because this state has not chosen to participate in the Medicaid program.

I urge the Ohio Assembly to adopt a Medicaid program in its next session to cover those families whose yearly income does not exceed $4,500. This is just above the poverty line level, and any family in that income category which incurs a serious illness will almost certainly become dependent upon public support.

Housing. The Commission conducted a special study of the housing problems of people of low income in the city. It has come up with recommendations which I believe will be helpful.

My Department of Community Development and other members of my staff are working on a legislative program to increase the capacity of the city to rehabilitate substandard housing, to build new housing, and to protect renters in homes where the codes are violated.

I will be presenting this package of legislation to the Legislature next year and I hope it will be passed.

A State Welfare Board. In accordance with the Commission's recommendation, I call upon the Governor to create a State Welfare Board immediately. This board should have representation of clients themselves along with people professionally qualified to evaluate the state welfare program and to make recommendations for its improvement. *I believe the Governor has the power to create such a board by executive order, but if legislation is required, I shall request the Legislature to enact this authorization.*

COUNTY LEVEL RECOMMENDATIONS

With respect to the recommendations at the county level, I am very glad to see that the County Welfare Department, under the direction of Eugene Burns, has already begun to put into effect some of the Commission's key recommendations. These include the utilization of affidavits rather than the wasteful and inefficient investigation procedures. It also includes appropriate steps to separate delivery of payments from provision of social services.

In addition, the county has begun to decentralize its welfare offices on a neighborhood basis. It is seeking state authorization for a number of additional basic improvements in welfare administration. *I intend for the city to cooperate more vigorously than heretofore with the county. We must ensure more effective as well as more efficient service to the poor in our city.*

CITY LEVEL RECOMMENDATIONS

From the point of view of the city itself, I have instructed Mr. Hill, Director of the proposed Department of Human and

Economic Resources, to take responsibility for representing the interests of the city's welfare clientele in accordance with the Commission's recommendation.

The Council for Economic Opportunity. The report recommended that action be taken to revitalize the Council for Economic Opportunity and make it more responsive to the needs of welfare clients. I have appointed 10 public officials to serve as representatives from the public sector. A number of new representatives from the poverty areas have been elected. And additional representatives of private agencies are coming on the Council's Board of Directors.

I expect them to invigorate the agency and to pay particular attention to ensuring that residents of poverty areas determine their own ends in the delivery of social services.

Multiservice Centers. The Commission recommended the establishment of multipurpose health and social service centers in neighborhoods through the city and emphasized again the importance of involving residents more effectively in the operation of such centers. *We have under way as part of* CLEVELAND NOW! *the creation of 10 multiservice centers which will provide a wide range of health and social services readily available on a neighborhood basis.*

This effort is moving on two fronts. We are working directly with the administrators of all major service agencies and also with a broad cross section of representatives from the various neighborhoods.

Education. Some of the most important recommendations of the Commission's report deal with the problems of education, particularly for the children in poverty areas. The time is right for a searching examination of fundamental methods for improving the system of education to deal with the kinds of problems highlighted by the Commission's report.

I will ask the Board of Education and the Superintendent of Schools to call a high-level conference to plan for a major attack on the whole area of school problems as they relate to welfare recipients and the disadvantaged generally. Representatives of a cross section of the community should be involved in this conference. It would be specifically charged with charting the steps to be taken now for desegregation, decentralization, and revised educational procedures, along with teacher retraining.

With respect to the specific needs of school children on welfare, I trust that any practices which would cause embarrassment to welfare children have been effectively removed. I know that the Board of Education is conscious of this problem and has taken appropriate measures.

Employment. The Commission devoted a great deal of attention to the problems of employment, including training, wages, protection of working mothers, and a variety of other features of the manpower and employment situation. The Commission has exploded the myth that the cure for welfare is merely employment. The public welfare rolls are made up predominantly of people who are outside the labor market. Ninety-seven per cent are either children under 18, aged or disabled persons, or mothers and grandmothers caring for dependent children.

It is, nevertheless, extremely important to enhance the capacities of those on welfare who might become employable—to enlarge their opportunities for self-maintenance. With greater availability of job opportunities—both to Negroes and whites—we can expect more men to stay and support their families. *My administration will press hard to strengthen the various programs for recruitment, training, and educational employment opportunities.*

The Voluntary Effort. It has been a noteworthy feature of the Cleveland community that over the years the United Appeal has been enthusiastically supported. I personally want to see the United Appeal supported to the hilt. *I want its resources to increase with the understanding that a large share of the funds must be devoted to the inner city, particularly to the poverty areas of the inner city.*

I understand that both the Cleveland Welfare Federation and the United Appeal have such intentions. *On this premise, I strongly support the efforts of the United Appeal to increase its goal and achieve success.*

Follow-up. To ensure the vigorous follow-up of the recommendations of the Commission's report, I intend to mobilize the community to implement them now.

I am appointing an Urban Coalition composed of high-level leadership from every major sector of the Cleveland community. I shall request the Coalition to give high priority to the follow-up of the Commission recommendations and to report to me on progress being made.

The Commission has my earnest thanks. It has earned the profound appreciation of this community.

September 11, 1968   CARL B. STOKES, MAYOR

CONTENTS

Foreword v

Preface: Response by Mayor Carl B. Stokes to the Report of The Mayor's Commission on the Crisis in Welfare xi

PART I. OVERVIEW

1. *The Crisis in Welfare* 3
   - The Crisis of the Welfare Recipient 3
   - Major Recommendations of the Commission 5
   - Today's Poverty 7
   - Welfare and Employment 9
   - The State of Ohio and Welfare Needs 12
   - Spending for Welfare 15
   - Conclusion 16

PART II. FINDINGS AND RECOMMENDATIONS

2. *The Welfare System and Its Funding* 19
   - Standards for Assistance Payments 19
   - National Minimum Income 23
   - Health and Welfare Levy 26
   - State Income Tax 26
   - Welfare Administration—Eligibility and Service 29
   - The Need for a Simplified Manual 37
   - Fair Hearings for Welfare Clients 38
   - Decentralization of Services 41
   - County Welfare Advisory Board 42
   - State Welfare Advisory Board 43

City Representative for Welfare 43
Social Security Amendments of 1967 44
A Bill of Rights for Welfare Clients—A
  General Statement of the Commission... 45

3. *Employment and Training* 48
  Job Training, Employment Standards, and
    Entry-Pay Levels 51
  Racial Discrimination in Employment
    and in Craft Unions 52
  Community Service Employment Projects
    for the Unemployed 52
  Development of Industry in Depressed Areas 52
  Transportation 53
  Employment of Women 53
  Employment of AFDC Mothers 54
  Day Care Facilities for Working Mothers .. 54
  Service Industry Employment Programs ... 55
  Youth Employment 55
  Follow-up and Supportive Services for
    Special Manpower Programs 56

4. *Education* 57
  Funding 60
  Experimentation 61
  Training of Teachers 61
  Community Role of School Personnel 61
  School System Advocacy, Program
    Coordination, and Community
    Relations 62
  Equitable Treatment of Recipients 62
  School Lunch Program 62
  Expanded Use of Title I Funds 63
  School Library Fees 63

5. *Health* 64
  The Health Problems of Welfare Clients ... 64
  Establishment of Newly Structured and
    Financed Joint City-County
    Health Department 66

B. Myths and Realities in Welfare 95
C. Poverty and Unemployment in Cleveland 104
D. National Expenditures for Public Assistance from State and Local Funds, Fiscal Year 1967 124
E. Share of Cost of Public Assistance Programs by Levels of Government 126
F. Tables of Standard Allowances for Food, Clothing, Personal Expenses, and Utilities 127
G. Some Caseload Data on Public Welfare in Cuyahoga County 130
H. Note on Illegitimacy 132
I. Fact Sheet, Issue 6, Cuyahoga County Welfare Department, 1968 133
J. Excerpt from Memorandum on Presumptive Eligibility and Welfare Assistance, by Professor Nathan D. Grundstein 136
K. Form Used by the Cuyahoga County Welfare Department for General Relief and All Emergencies 139
L. Table of Organization, Cuyahoga County Welfare Department 141
M. Application for Fair Hearing, Prescribed by Ohio State Department of Public Welfare, Division of Social Administration 142
N. Comparison of Age and Employment Status of Cuyahoga County Recipients and National Recipients, 1967 143
O. Employment and Training 144
P. Social Security Amendments of 1967 154
Q. Miscellaneous Tables 159
R. Social Problem Index 169
S. Substandard Housing Units, City of Cleveland, 1960 171
T. Areas of Underemployment or Unemployment, City of Cleveland, 1967 172

SELECTED BIBLIOGRAPHY 173

TABLES

2.1	A Comparison Between the Cleveland AFDC Monthly Budget for a Family of Four and the Adequate Budget Developed by the Community Council of Greater New York	21
B.1	Internal Revenue Frauds, 1959	99
C.1	A Profile of Social Characteristics for Target Areas	114
C.2	Youth Population of City of Cleveland, by Age, Race, and Poverty Level	115
C.3	Comparison of Annual Dropout Rates in Title I and Non-Title I Senior High Schools	116
C.4a	Youth, by Age and Poverty Level, for Kinsman and East Central Target Areas	117
C.4b	Youth, by Age and Poverty Level, for Hough and Glenville Target Areas	118
C.4c	Youth, by Age and Poverty Level, for Near West Side and West Central Target Areas	119
C.5	Aid to Families with Dependent Children, City of Cleveland, for Selected Neighborhoods	120
C.6	Median Incomes of Nonwhite Families in Selected Areas	121
C.7	Status of Youth, 16–21, in Selected Social Planning Areas, 1966 (Estimated)	122
C.8	Incidence of Poverty Among Negro Female-Headed Households, 1959 and 1964, by Selected Target Areas	123
C.9	Male Juvenile Delinquency, Ages 12–17, by Selected Target Areas	123
D.1	National Expenditures for Public Assistance from State and Local Funds, Fiscal Year 1967	124
F.1	Standard Allowances to Cover Food, Clothing, and Personal Expenses, Effective July 1, 1967	127

F.2	Maximum Allowance for Housing, Including Utilities (Class I Counties)	128
F.3	Allowances for Utilities when Not Included in Rent.	129
G.1	Caseload, Cuyahoga County Welfare Department, 1967	130
G.2	Growth of AFDC Program, 1957–67	130
G.3	Expenditures of Cuyahoga County Welfare Department, 1967	131
Q.1a	Comparison of Public and Voluntary Funds for Social Insurances, Veterans Programs and Welfare, and Health, Recreation, and Other Services in Cleveland, by Field of Service and Source of Funds, 1965	160
Q.1b	Services Included Under Social Insurances, Veterans Programs and Welfare, and Health, Welfare, Recreation, and Other Services	161
Q.2	Percentage Distribution of Funds for Welfare, Health, and Recreation Services, by Field of Service and Source of Funds in Cleveland, 1965	163
Q.3	Estimates of Population of Cuyahoga County, 1965, by Poverty and Nonpoverty Areas	164
Q.4	Distribution of Funds by Voluntary and Public Welfare Agencies, Cuyahoga County, 1966	165
Q.5a	Distribution of Clients Served by Voluntary and Public Welfare Agencies, by Function and Area, 1966	165
Q.5b	Agencies Included in Voluntary and Public Welfare Services, by Function	167
R.1	Social Problem Index, by Selected Social Planning Areas	169

CHARTS

Chart 2.1 Comparative 1968 Monthly Budgets for an Urban Family of Four on Public Assistance. 22
App. L. Table of Organization, Cuyahoga County Welfare Department 141
App. N. Comparison of Age and Employment Status of Cuyahoga County Recipients and National Recipients, 1967 143
App. S. Substandard Housing Units, City of Cleveland, 1960 171
App. T. Areas of Underemployment or Unemployment, City of Cleveland, 1967 172

PART I
OVERVIEW

1. THE CRISIS IN WELFARE

THE CRISIS OF THE WELFARE RECIPIENT

The dream that some have had of welfare adequately providing for the needy has become a nightmare to the recipient. The welfare client lives in the midst of the Affluent Society and the Good Life, but he is resigned to the Poorhouse Society and the Bitter Life.

What is welfare, in human terms, to the client? It is attempting to sell blood to buy a child toys at Christmas and being turned away for being anemic. It is a child wearing $1 tennis shoes through the winter. It is selling food stamps to buy sanitary napkins and toothpaste. It is covering one's mouth to hide missing teeth.

Persons on welfare cannot carry life insurance beyond $500. Relatively few can carry that much. If someone dies, there is no allowance for burial. The family can either accept a pauper's burial or scrounge for money to pay funeral expenses. A pauper's burial is considered the final human indignity, and many families will go to any length to provide at least some kind of private burial. Life insurance up to a small maximum amount may now be kept, but there is no allowance for it.

On Saturday night, July 18, 1966, a 26-year-old mother died of a heart attack. She and her children had been supported by the Aid to Families with Dependent Children public assistance program. She had had little during life, but her friends would see to it that she would at least be buried with dignity—not by means of the $80 pauper burial made possible by the City of Cleveland's Health Department and paid by the city after determining "indigency," but by donations collected in the community.

No one knew it then, but the common practice among the

poor of collecting dimes and quarters to finance the burial of the impoverished—a final symbol of protest of the poor that their lives, indeed, had some meaning—was to be one of the sparks that set the Hough area afire for five days of rioting, during which five persons were killed and hundreds injured.

One of the burial fund collection points was the Seventy-Niner's Café at East 79th Street and Hough Avenue. The sequence of events remains clouded, but one of the welfare clients seeking donations for the burial was ejected from the Seventy-Niner. The treatment she received aroused the resentment of black men in the bar, and the first spark of the Hough riots was struck.

The indignity of the burial policy of the welfare system for many years had no meaning or effect—except upon those directly involved. But in a complex society the injustices mount until the revulsion erupts blindly and touches us all, sometimes through violence.

Unable or unwilling to perceive the cause and effect of indignity and the harsh reaction and possible violence it breeds, we perpetuate inequities at a time in history when the backlog of injustice is high and the sensitivity to it acute. The report of the President's National Advisory Commission on Civil Disorders has detailed the consequences.

The restrictive portions of the 1967 Social Security Act Amendments will be implemented in such a climate. Their eventual effect, as with the burial policy, remains unknown. But, as Dr. George Wiley, Director of the Poverty Rights Action Center, the national organization of the welfare rights movement, told our Commission, "The man related to the welfare mother is not going to sit idly by and see black women brutalized."

The punitive nature of the Social Security Amendments of 1967 is aimed at blacks in the ghetto, Dr. Wiley warns, and, when they are applied locally, people might not know the name of the law but will feel its results and react.

No one can tell how many other welfare inequities, and their related demeaning attitudes are building resentment that eventually will be released—how and upon whom remains unpredictable. But a society that ignores the warning does so at its peril.

The welfare rolls include elderly, blind, and disabled persons, but the real target of the controversy which surrounds public welfare is the young family on Aid to Families with Dependent Children (AFDC). In the large cities, such as Cleveland, most of these families are Negro, a fact which is closely related to the discrimination often shown to recipients of this form of aid. It should be noted, however, that in the nation as a whole most recipients of public assistance are white, including those on AFDC. According to the National Center for Social Statistics, the estimates[1] for mid-1968 of the proportion of those on public assistance who are Negro are the following:

Old Age Assistance	22%
Aid to Families with Dependent Children	49%
Aid to the Blind	29%
Aid to the Physically Disabled	31%
OVER-ALL	40%

To be poor in a rich society is bad. To be black and poor is worse. The child on AFDC bears an added weight, for he often feels rebuffed by society, even by those institutions designed to help him. But the heart of the problem is the level of assistance which keeps recipients in abject poverty, deprives them of dignity, and weakens both the incentive and the capacity of the young to equip themselves for economic independence.

MAJOR RECOMMENDATIONS OF THE COMMISSION

The Commission's work has resulted in a long list of recommendations, but those that are major and fundamental, on which most of the others rest, are the following:

1. A national program of income guarantees and supplements is recommended, assuring a budgetary standard at least at the federally determined "poverty level" for all needy families and individuals—and as soon as possible at a higher level of adequacy—with a policy of guaranteed employment for all who can work, the federal government being the employer of last resort.

2. While the present system of public welfare is with us,

---

[1] Provided in telephone conversation with Dr. Stein by Dr. Robert H. Mugge, Acting Director, National Center for Social Statistics, Social and Rehabilitation Service, Department of Health, Education, and Welfare.

the State of Ohio should immediately base all public assistance grants on a minimum of the nationally determined poverty level (currently $3,335 for a family of four).

3. To help finance such a program, as well as needed support for health and education and other purposes, a state income tax should be instituted.

4. The following series of administrative recommendations for county welfare have been designed to enhance the dignity and capacity for self-reliance of the welfare recipient and to protect his rights:

   a) Establish the poor person's eligibility for relief through his filling out an affidavit or declaration of income, with sample checking of accuracy as with income tax returns, rather than retain the demeaning and wasteful case-by-case investigation of clients' resources.
   b) Separate the client's eligibility for financial help from his access to service. He should be free to utilize the services he needs without reporting to the person who also determined his eligibility for assistance. This should have the effect also of freeing the social workers to be helpful without having to assume the role of investigators.
   c) Clarify and strengthen the fair hearing process so that clients can have their grievances properly adjudicated.

5. Congress should immediately repeal the freeze on AFDC caseloads, and the other restrictive 1967 amendments to the Social Security Act.

6. A representative advisory committee should be established for the State Welfare Board; a more representative and reactivated advisory committee should be established for the County Welfare Department; and the Mayor of Cleveland should designate a special staff person to be concerned solely with welfare problems.

7. The State Legislature should take immediate steps to broaden the coverage of the Title XIX program to include *all* medically indigent families.

8. Voluntary agencies should establish public welfare committees coordinated by the Public Welfare Committee of the Welfare Federation, on which welfare clients of the latter committee would be represented. Voluntary health and welfare agencies should allocate an increasing share of their resources to ensure that a more adequate system of welfare assistance and social services is available to all.

In order to implement these and other recommendations,

the Commission urges the establishment of an ongoing citizen effort, independent of political commitments, and adequately financed and composed of the kind of cross section of citizens which has comprised the membership of the Commission.

TODAY'S POVERTY[2]

The poverty of today is different from that of the days of the depression of the 1930's when millions were unemployed. Those who were poor then were indeed very poor, and it was tragic. But because this was a mass phenomenon, the stigma of being poor was not as acute when there was a feeling of identity with the millions of others who were in the same position. There was also the prospect of moving up and out as economic conditions changed and governmental programs could be launched to remedy the more acute sources of distress.

Even then, the attitudes long held in our country that anyone who was poor or not employed had something essentially wrong with him, were still very prevalent. This is an attitude that continues to exist even though the facts show that it is totally unjustified. As soon as jobs became available, particularly with the outbreak of World War II, mass relief rolls suddenly dwindled. Unlike today, the relief rolls included the employable who were poor because there was no work to be had. When there was employment, everyone who could work went to work. Virtually no one preferred to be on welfare rather than to be self-supporting. Exactly the same situation has prevailed throughout our history and is still true today—except that today the percentage of employable men receiving public assistance is under 3%.

Our society is characterized by affluence. Our poverty is not that which characterizes many of the developing countries of the world, nor is it the highly visible mass-unemployment poverty of the 1930's in our country. The poor of today, as has been impressed upon us repeatedly during these last few years, are often invisible, particularly if one's life centers around the suburbs and the business and entertainment areas in the cities. It is a poverty characterized by degradation.

There are many kinds of poor and many reasons for poverty. There are those who are poor because they are aged and have

---

[2]Adapted from "Public Welfare—Public Scapegoat," address by Herman D. Stein to the City Club of Cleveland, March 1, 1968.

no resources; who are poor because they are physically unable to work; or who have been hit hard by discrimination and absence of opportunity for adequate schooling and jobs, or have come from backgrounds where this was true. There are pockets of poverty in areas of the country which industrialization has passed by—neglected areas such as Appalachia—and there is the poverty that results from unemployment due to automation.

A recent estimate indicates that about 32 million persons in the United States live at a level below the poverty line. Of these, about 9 million receive public assistance. For an area such as the Cleveland area, the poverty line is now $3,335 per year for a family of four, and most people in the poverty category are well below this standard.

In the State of Ohio, for example, the total received by a family of four under the Aid to Families with Dependent Children budget is approximately $2,316 a year, or about $1,000 below what is estimated by the federal government as the barest minimum necessary for health and decency. In contrast, the U.S. Department of Labor established that a moderate budget for the average city worker with the same size family in Cleveland would be about $8,400.

One can easily get lost in the complexities of finances for the various programs in welfare: Aid for the Aged, Aid to the Blind, General Assistance, Aid to Dependent Children, and so forth.[3] Some illustrative information of the dimensions of the problem as faced by welfare families may, however, be in order.

In 1959, the State of Ohio established a minimum subsistence standard of 90 cents per day per child. As late as July 31, 1967, payments for children on AFDC were still pegged at 73 cents per day. It is now 83 cents. This is supposed to take care of every need except rent. It is supposed to take care of food, clothing, carfare, school expenses, toothpaste, etc. This is simply not possible.

Calculations for family budgets on relief are not easy. They are made individually and are affected by a number of factors, such as the age and sex of the children. A chance error, indeed, can be a matter of agony for a family until it is corrected later. But it would be fairly typical that an entire family of four on

---

[3]See Appendix G for a statistical summary of welfare programs administered by the county.

Aid to Dependent Children would receive about $25 a week for all expenses after rent and utilities. If the utilities come to more than the allowance, which is often the case, the food money may go for that purpose to prevent eviction. It is not uncommon for families with children to have their gas cut off in freezing weather for nonpayment of utility bills.

People wonder why there was a crisis for children this winter. There has been a crisis every winter. Hundreds of mothers have gone without adequate clothing themselves so that something could be supplied for their children. Occasionally, some clothing supplies can be obtained from special school resources, but these resources are meager and uneven and the distribution difficult. That these AFDC mothers can manage at all is a tribute to their incredible resourcefulness and their will to survive.

According to a study by the Nutrition Association of Greater Cleveland, there is strong evidence that many children on welfare are living on inadequate, substandard diets. Lack of funds forces many families to live almost exclusively on beans and rice a few weeks after receiving their welfare payment. It is no wonder that so many of these children cannot afford the sneakers and the gym pants required at school, cannot contribute pennies to collections in school, often cannot purchase even the minimum required for school supplies, or participate in extracurricular school activities that require money! We talk about breaking the poverty cycle, and, rightly, about the importance of education, but our standard for support of these children leaves many of them without the physical energy to take advantage of schooling and sometimes with permanent scars from the indignities leveled at them for being different and unable to meet minimum expectations of dress or equipment.

As the Report of the President's National Advisory Commission on Civil Disorders stated: "Social welfare programs are basically designed to save money rather than to save people. And the tragedy is that all too often they end up doing neither." This view had also been expressed by Mitchell I. Ginsberg, former Commissioner of Social Services for New York City.

WELFARE AND EMPLOYMENT

Welfare is one of the less popular causes in American life. Nobody really likes it. Certainly those who have to take it don't like it. The social work profession doesn't like it. The taxpayers don't like it. There are strong appeals for basic change in proposals such as the negative income tax and other measures for a guaranteed minimum income, including children's allowances and expanded forms of Social Security, to subsidize those whose income falls below the official poverty standard, as well as abolition of the means test. Basic changes will develop, and we must keep thinking about the best kinds of changes to produce and then press forward to such reform. *But right now welfare is a necessity, and we have to make it work as best we can so long as the lives and well-being of people depend on it.*

Our society has never trusted the poor and particularly those who have to receive economic help. There has always been a strong feeling that there must be something wrong with someone who cannot maintain himself. We have come to realize, however, that in welfare costs we are simply paying a price, and too small a price at that, for our own society's weaknesses, lags, and failures. We are paying a price for decades of absence of adequate opportunity for education and jobs, for discrimination, for failure to invest massively in low-cost housing, for turning aside and not seeing the dire problems of the poverty-stricken until we are compelled to do so. In part, this inaction on our part results from the powerlessness of the poor, particularly of those who are on welfare. Partly it has been a matter of their invisibility to those whose way of life never brings them into contact with the poor, or who prefer to turn away.

Because of their powerlessness, and because of the unpopularity of welfare, welfare clients and welfare systems have been a ready target for every kind of misinformation that is circulated. Most prevalent among these is the notion that people on welfare could work and support themselves if they wanted to, but that they are really lazy and depend on the rest of us.

The facts are that, for the public assistance caseload as a whole, right here in Cuyahoga County as elsewhere, over 96% of all welfare recipients are unemployable; 64% are underage, 18% are mothers or grandmothers caring for children full-time, and the balance are aged people, many of whom are in nursing homes, and people who are permanently and totally disabled. Only 3% of those receiving public assistance are unemployed able-bodied fathers.[4]

---

[4]See Appendix B for a fuller discussion of this and other "Myths and Realities."

For anyone on welfare who may have potential for self-support or self-help there is a work training program. This is the Title V Work Training Program, which includes 40 hours weekly for training or work experience. Eugene Burns, the Director of the County Welfare Department, reported that 75% of those who failed in the training program failed because of recurring physical and mental illnesses. In the AIM Job Training Program, it has been found that a high percentage of the young trainees have physical illnesses, many of them traceable to poor nutrition.

Single men and couples with no children who are considered employable by the County Welfare Department cannot receive any public assistance. These people work at any jobs that are available, usually at substandard wages. A large proportion of mothers on public assistance would much prefer work to relief. The major deterrent to these mothers is the problem of providing day care for their children. The kind of jobs available to these mothers and the small amount of payment they receive is also a grievous problem.

The last national studies indicate that at any one time, about 4% to 5% of children in the nation under 18 are receiving Aid to Families with Dependent Children. However, the turnover rate is very high, primarily because, when employment is available to the heads of these families, they go off relief. The best estimate of how many children might be receiving AFDC payments at some time of their lives in the nation as a whole is one in six.

Joseph Califano, Jr., assistant to President Lyndon B. Johnson, reported that a special study for the President revealed that "less than 1 per cent" of the nation's 7.3 million welfare clients in 1967 were employable. The report stated that only 50,000 of these Americans would be capable of getting off welfare—even if every program, private and public, were adequately staffed and efficiently operated.

Of the 7.3 million, the report showed that: 2.1 million, mostly women, are more than 65 years of age; 3.5 million are children whose parents cannot afford to support them; 1 million are parents (about 900,000 are mothers); 700,000 are either blinded or so severely handicapped that their work potential, if any, is extremely limited; 50,000 are trainable, but the programs for training are not available, nor are they expected to be.

The Commission reported the following breakdown on those receiving welfare in Cuyahoga County:

64% are children under the age of 18;
18% are mothers or grandmothers caring for dependent children;
10% are elderly (many in nursing homes) and out of the labor force permanently;
4.5% are permanently or totally disabled and/or blind;
3% (approximately) are unemployed males.

These statistics may not tell the entire story. Indeed, they do not tell the human story. But without them it would be impossible to weigh the problem and suggest possible solutions. The figures do suggest what most people are not ready to accept, but what similar studies show and social workers long have known: *Most people receiving public assistance cannot enter the American labor market today.*

Here is a sober statement made by a research analyst of the U.S. Department of Health, Education, and Welfare: "The descriptive data available on public assistance recipients lead to the general conclusion that even with the best possible services, only about 5% at most of the recipients can be helped to the point of self-sufficiency within a reasonable length of time." He also points out, however, that this 5% would consist mainly of AFDC parents and, since they have an average of 3.1 children, if they were all helped to get off relief, there might be a reduction of 20% in the total caseload. "It must be recognized as a delusion that any great dent can be made in the near future in the over-all assistance population through job rehabilitation, since this is by and large a handicapped population."[5] The only hope for the assistance population relates to the children.

THE STATE OF OHIO AND WELFARE NEEDS

Two legislative sessions ago, the Ohio Legislature, upon the

---

[5] Robert H. Mugge, "Demographic Analysis and Public Assistance" (mimeographed). Prepared for the Annual Meeting of the Population Association of America, New York City, April 30, 1966. Quoted by permission of the author, who is now Acting Director, National Center for Social Statistics, Department of Health, Education, and Welfare, and was at the time of writing with the Bureau of Family Services, Welfare Administration.

initiative of Governor James Rhodes, established a new financing formula to meet the costs of public welfare needs.

Under this formula, the nonfederal cost of financing welfare (the federal government pays two-thirds of the cost) would be paid on the basis of 90% by the state and 10% by the county. To establish this formula the county was required to give up the income it had been receiving from the public utilities tax.

During this time, the state had set a minimum standard required by welfare families to live in health and decency. However, the state did not meet its own standard, paying only 76% of what it deemed minimum.

In the legislative session of 1967—again under the leadership of Governor Rhodes—the state reneged on its own financing formula by requiring a *new* state-county sharing arrangement to bring the standard up to 100% of the minimum needs the state had set. Under this new formula, additional costs to bring the standard up to 100% were on the basis of one-third from the state and two-thirds from the county, not the previously legislated formula of 90-10. However, the state did not return to the county any of the public utilities tax income it had acquired in the prior session.

The new formula did not serve to bring standards up to the 100% of even the grossly inadequate minimum set by the state. Indeed, the state had to pay almost none of the funds it put aside to meet the new 2 to 1 ratio of cost, since only three small counties—and none where the need was greatest—were able to meet the new cost ratio.

For example, Cuyahoga County, in which Cleveland is located, would have had to increase its share by about $6 million to raise its two-thirds of the formula, while it had given up $4 million in public utilities taxes on the basis of the 90-10 formula, which had been discarded by the new arrangement.

The U.S. Commission on Civil Rights concluded after a study of the welfare payments problem in Cuyahoga County in 1966 that "as measured by the Ohio State minimum standard of living and other objective standards, cash payments under the A[F]DC program in Cuyahoga County are GROSSLY INADEQUATE TO PROVIDE SUPPORT AND CARE REQUISITE FOR HEALTH AND DECENCY."

Two years later, the situation shows no improvement. The victims of the state government's attitude are primarily children. The Governor and the Ohio Legislature have not heeded the warnings. The Governor did not respond to the visits of a number of eminent citizens from Cleveland and elsewhere to urge a reconsideration of his policy. In the legislative session early in 1968 a bill was introduced by Senators Taft and Jackson to release $8.6 million that had been appropriated for Aid to Families with Dependent Children. If this were released, $2.4 million could have been expended for the AFDC program in Cuyahoga County. A wire was sent to Governor Rhodes by Mayor Stokes, followed by a letter from the County Commissioners and the Mayor's Commission on the Crisis in Welfare, urging that the Governor take leadership in having these funds released as quickly as possible for their intended purposes. It was pointed out that this was not a political issue and that what was under consideration was provision for children who are currently allowed an average of no more than 83 cents a day to take care of food, clothing, school supplies, carfare, and all of the other requirements for the most minimal level of living.

The Governor did not act and the bill remained in committee.

The Mayor's Commission on the Crisis in Welfare had meanwhile recommended that an increase of 1 mill in the county's health and welfare levy be placed before the voters in the May, 1968, primary so that matching funds from the state could be raised to increase present welfare payments closer to the standard established by the state itself in 1966. The County Commissioners voted to place this increase before the voters, and fortunately it was passed. Although the increased millage will have to be used for certain health and welfare purposes beyond the increase in AFDC standards, the commitment made by the County Commissioners to the Mayor's Commission was that the major proportion of the increased revenues will be devoted to raising the relief allowance.

The passage of the levy does not, however, reduce in any way the urgent necessity of releasing funds now tied up by the State of Ohio. The continued retention of these funds represents, in the minds of the Commission, a callous disregard of the desperate conditions of tens of thousands of destitute children in Cuyahoga County and in the state as a whole.

The State of Ohio has shown virtually no initiative in dealing with the problems of the poor and has turned a deaf ear to representatives of the Welfare Federation of Cleveland as well as to welfare clients themselves. Ohio ranks 34th among the states in per capita expenditures for public assistance; it ranks 16th in per capita income for its citizens.

It is high time for this deplorable situation to change and for Ohio to assume its proper responsibilities. A number of the recommendations in this report urge the state to take certain specific measures. Not all of these involve new revenues but they all require an attitude of concern on the part of the state authorities that has not yet been evident towards the plight of the poor, specifically, the poor who require public assistance.

SPENDING FOR WELFARE

Support for the poor who have no other alternatives and are out of the labor market will require more funds than have yet been made available. This report makes recommendations for the source of these funds, particularly through tax revenues. But all such recommendations confront public reluctance to spend for welfare.

Implicit in the argument against spending for welfare is the public feeling that no one should be subsidized, i.e., that everyone should earn his own way. Those making this argument assume that they are not subsidized but are completely self-reliant. They don't consider as subsidy, Federal Housing Administration insured loans, student college loans by the federal government, government contracts to firms which employ them, massive farm subsidies, federal subsidy of highways and airlines, and a host of other indirect subsidies the poor do not enjoy.

Ironically, a recent poll by Representative Frances P. Bolton in the 22nd Congressional District, an area made up primarily of middle- and upper-income families, clearly shows the inconsistency of the argument against government subsidy of society's needs. Of all District 22 voters polled, 69% favored a cutback in domestic spending to reduce the need for an income tax increase. Domestic programs, it should be understood, is a euphemism for programs for the poor. Thus, these voters showed they were against "subsidization" of programs for the poor. Yet, 66% of the same voters, when asked if they favored tax credits for college education expenses, favored this proposal. Thus, they were willing to have government subsidization of themselves but not the poor.

The vast government subsidies of middle- and upper-income families and of business and industry are taken routinely as not only necessary but deserved. Just the opposite reaction greets

programs to help the economically disadvantaged.
Herein lies part of the crisis in welfare.

CONCLUSION

The Commission, in preparing this report, has analyzed, studied, and researched much of what has been documented in similar studies. The ills are the same, the measures of cure by now are familiar. The answers, unfortunately, have become clichés by constant repetition.

The history of report-making is a clear warning that this report, like others, may go largely ignored, whatever its quality, and despite the effort to detail some constructive directions for change. Much stronger watchdog efforts, much more resolute political activity, and much more involvement of the private sector than we have yet seen will be needed to pursue such recommendations towards implementation. Certain channels for making this possible have been suggested, but, if past history is a guide, they can be effective only if there is a truly informed and aroused citizenry.

PART II
FINDINGS AND RECOMMENDATIONS

2. THE WELFARE SYSTEM AND ITS FUNDING

STANDARDS FOR ASSISTANCE PAYMENTS

The issue of society's having responsibility to provide people in need with a humane, minimum standard of subsistence is fraught with confusion and ideological differences. The idea of government's providing poor people with a basic floor of health and decency, as a matter of right, has been seen as a violation of American virtues ever since this concept was included in the Social Security Act of 1935. After careful investigation, the Mayor's Commission on the Crisis in Welfare concurs with the findings of the National Advisory Commission on Civil Disorders, which found the welfare system deficient in two critical ways in relation to the level of payments:

> First, it excludes a large number of persons who are in great need, and who, if provided a decent level of support, might be able to become more productive and self-sufficient;
> Second, for those who are included, it provides assistance well below the minimum necessary for a decent level of existence, and imposes restrictions that encourage continued dependency on welfare and undermine self-respect.[1]

Below, three levels of payments are described. The first two have been cited as representing adequate minimum standards of health and decency. The Mayor's Commission believes these minimum standards are grossly inadequate and recommends the adoption of a new standard.

Ohio Minimum Standard for Health and Decency. In 1959 the Ohio Department of Welfare attempted to design a budget

---

[1]*Report of the National Advisory Commission on Civil Disorders,* Government Printing Office, Washington, 1968, p. 457.

that reflected what authorities in different budget areas considered to be a minimum level of health and decency. The budget included such items as food, shelter, utilities, clothing, and school and household supplies. Age, sex, and size of family were also taken into consideration.[2] Despite the fact that the budget was designated as minimum, the state has never met its own standard for AFDC families. In 1959, the minimum standard for a family of four (a mother and three children) was $201 per month. Today, nine years later, the state has still not reached its own 1959 standard despite the substantial increase in the cost of living. Ohio now pays $193, or 83% of its own standard of $232, compared with 85% of its standard in 1959. Moreover, the standard of 1959 was based on a differential age breakdown which has now been eliminated, causing further economic discrimination against families with children under 8 years of age.

For the family of four on a budget of $193 per month, $70 may be applied to rent and $20 to utilities, leaving only $103 a month, or less than $25 a week for food, clothing, transportation, school supplies, and all other incidentals. (For a detailed description of how a typical family spends its $193 monthly allowance, see Appendix B, "Myth: The welfare budget in Ohio is adequate.")

The Federally Established Poverty Line. In 1965 the Social Security Administration developed a budget which specified that the minimum income required to support an average urban family of four was $3,130 per year. This standard has been adopted by the Office of Economic Opportunity as representing the minimum poverty line. Because of the increased cost of living, the poverty line was raised in 1968 to $3,335 by Social Security Administration economists. Thus a typical Ohio family of four on public assistance receives $2,316 per year, or approximately $1,000 less than the federal poverty line, exclusive of food stamps and medical service.

The Community Council of Greater New York Adequate Minimum Budget. In contrast to the Ohio minimum standard and the federally established poverty line, the Community Council of Greater New York in 1967 set forth an adequate mini-

---

[2]See Appendix F for tables of the state standard allowances.

mum budget of $6,251 a year for an urban family of four. This budget provides for the same items supposedly covered by the Ohio state budget and the federal poverty line budget but adds a number of items which have become essentials, such as medical care, life insurance, transportation, health and telephone service, laundry and clothing upkeep, replacement of household furnishings, reading materials, recreation, tobacco, gifts, and contributions.

This modest budget comes to $521 per month, or $6,251 per year. Table 2.1 compares the Cleveland AFDC budget for a family of four and the basic budget suggested by the Community Council of Greater New York, which represents a level of adequate decency. The wide range between a budget considered adequate by the Community Council and the amounts actually paid to an AFDC family in Ohio is graphically illustrated in Chart 2.1.

TABLE 2.1
A Comparison Between the Cleveland AFDC Monthly Budget for a Family of Four and the Adequate Budget Developed by the Community Council of Greater New York

	CLEVELAND AFDC BUDGET	COMMUNITY COUNCIL OF GREATER N.Y. BUDGET
Rent } Heat } Utilities }	$90	$102
Food } Clothing } Personal care }	103[a]	$257
Household supplies	—	4
House furnishings	—	17
Laundry	—	7
Medical	—	31
Transportation (non-car)	—	27
Reading materials, education, recreation, etc.	—	46
Telephone	—	6
Life insurance	—	9
Gifts, contributions	—	15
Total	$193	$521

[a]Food stamps increase purchase value by $30.

CHART 2.1
Comparative 1968 Monthly Budgets for an Urban Family of Four on Public Assistance

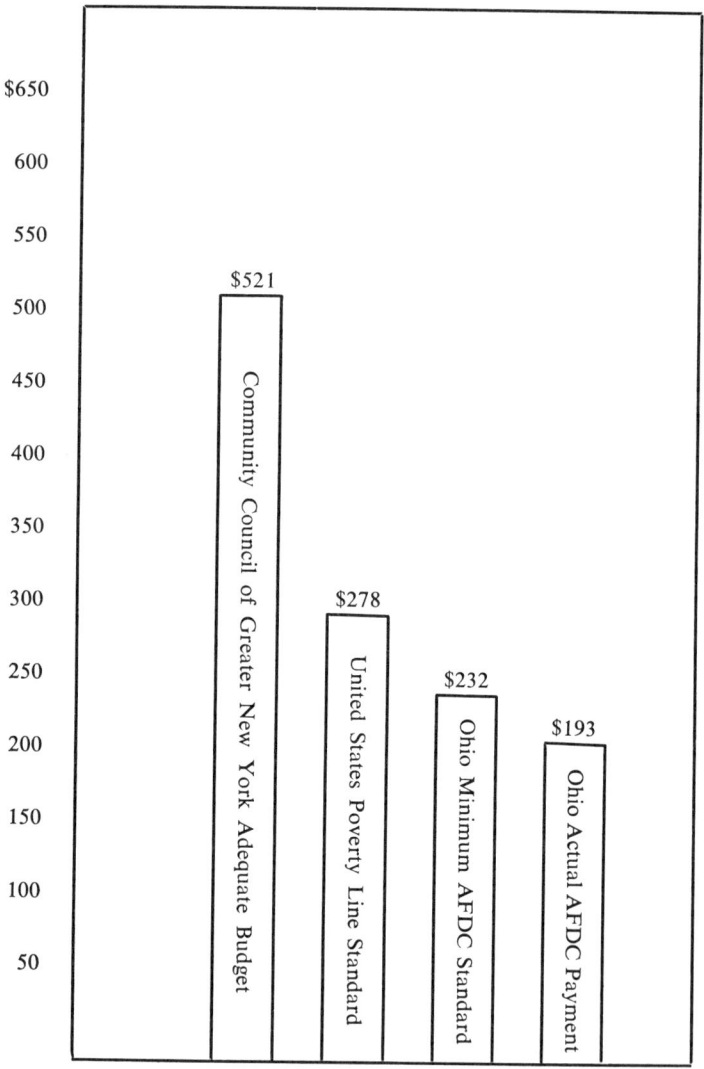

Establishment of a Comprehensive Neighborhood Health Center Program 67
Data Processing Centers for Health Records of the Medically Indigent 67
Establishment of a Joint Welfare-Health Services Training Program 68
Improvement of Health Services in the Schools 68
Definition of Responsibility of the Newly Established Comprehensive Health Planning Agency to Health Care of the Medically Indigent 69
Increase in Funds and Population Coverage of the Title XIX Program 70

6. *Housing* 71
   Increasing Public Housing Units 72
   Suburban Housing Opportunities 73
   Cleveland City Council 73
   Housing Code Enforcement 73
   State Legislation 74
   Advocacy for Tenants 74

7. *Public-Voluntary Relationships* 75

8. *Council for Economic Opportunity* 80

PART III. CONCLUSIONS

9. *Summary of Major Recommendations by Level* 85
   Federal 85
   State 85
   County 86
   City 87
   Private Sector 89
   Concluding Note 89

APPENDIXES

A. Letter from Mayor Carl B. Stokes, Appointing the Commission on the Crisis in Welfare .. 93

NATIONAL MINIMUM INCOME

Although the Mayor's Commission on the Crisis in Welfare recommends improvements in the welfare system to the extent we have to live with it, the Commission views the present method of public assistance as profoundly deficient and incapable of basic reform. It cannot meet the right of American families to live in health and economic dignity.

The public assistance program provides income far below desirable levels, excludes thousands of families in dire need, and inherently lacks a dignified relationship with clients. It is also needlessly costly as presently administered. Modest payment increases and administrative reform cannot alter the system's intrinsic failure.

In May of 1968, more than 1,000 academic economists, including such eminent scholars as Professors Paul A. Samuelson of the Massachusetts Institute of Technology, John Kenneth Galbraith of Harvard, James Tobin of Yale, and Harold Watts and Robert Lampman of the University of Wisconsin endorsed a "national system of income guarantees and supplements," noting that the cost of such a plan would be "substantial but well within the nation's economic and fiscal capacity.[3]

Thus, after extensive and careful examination of the present system, the Mayor's Commission concludes that a national minimum income, permitting a standard of decent and healthful living for all needy families and individuals, is necessary and desirable for the following reasons:

1. It would be efficient and simple to administer by an automated national system of income delivery, thus avoiding high administrative costs at various governmental levels and the indignities of present eligibility procedures.

2. It would provide benefits to all poor families, including the 22 million families below the poverty level and the 8 million on public assistance. This would relieve the federal government of its policy of maintaining public assistance below the poverty level by its own programs and establish clearly, as its policy, the elimination of poverty.

3. To those who object that such a program would destroy incentive to work we need only say that assurance of meaningful jobs and training programs to those who are employable

---
[3] *New York Times,* May 28, 1968, p. 1.

should be built into the program, with the governm nt as employer of last resort, if necessary.

4. The majority of persons receiving public assistance—the elderly, the disabled, the blind, children, and mothers taking care of children—are not employable. A decent level of living would enable the young to become more productive.

5. The Commission rejects the common criticism that workers will prefer indolence to a higher standard of living, not only because the formula to provide incentive would be built in, but evidence tells us income itself is an incentive to acquire more.

As James C. Vadakin, the economist, has written: "Witness the growing of multiple wage earners among American families; the widespread desire of employees for overtime work, and the fact that over recent decades, almost 60 per cent of our increased ability to produce has been taken in the form of more goods and services whereas only 40 per cent has gone to increased leisure."[4]

To the objection that a minimum income would cost too much, the Commission considers that the indirect costs of delinquency, dependency, disease, frustration, and hostility inherent in the present public assistance system far outweigh such costs. In actual dollars, a decent minimum standard for all needy families will produce dividends in productivity and taxes, rather than insuring further dependency as the present program does.

Estimates of cost range from $11 to $15 billion annually to bring needy families up to at least the present federally established poverty line level of $3,335. About $5.5 billion now spent for various categories of public assistance would be applied toward the cost. With the gross national product heading to $850 billion, the nation can well afford 1.5% to 1.8% of this amount to relieve poverty.

There are several widely endorsed plans for a suitable minimum income, including the negative income tax, a family allowance, and a national assistance standard for the states.

Under the negative income tax the federal government, through the income tax system, would pay the difference between a family's income and the minimum income required

---

[4]James C. Vadakin, "Critique of the Guaranteed Annual Income," *The Public Interest,* Spring, 1968, p. 61.

for a decent American standard of living. Incentives to work would be built in through a negative tax rate of 25% to 50%.

Under the family allowance system the federal government would provide an allowance to every family, with a fixed amount for each child, regardless of family need or income. This plan is often tied to a set of other benefits from Social Security, which would serve to maintain an income floor, particularly for families with children.[5]

Under a national assistance standard for the states, as recommended by the Advisory Council on Public Welfare in its 1966 report to the Secretary of Health, Education, and Welfare, a nationwide standard would be set, taking into account family size and circumstances for a "modest but adequate budget." Federal and state governments would cooperate, with the federal government paying the cost above a specified state share determined by each state's fiscal capacity.

Need would be the sole measure of eligibility and irrelevant exclusions such as age, family composition, residence, disability, and final responsibility would be eliminated. Social services would be available as a guaranteed right.

The Mayor's Commission is committed to the principle of national income maintenance. While it does not recommend one specific plan, the Commission leans toward the negative income tax as the most feasible and effective.

Recommendations

• As a first step for federal legislation in 1969, the Commission recommends the enactment by the Congress of a national program assuring a budget at the federally determined poverty line level (at least) for all needy families and individuals unable to work, and with a policy of guaranteed employment for all those able to work, the federal government being the employer of last resort. As soon as possible there should be national legislation to guarantee annual income for all Americans who earn less than an amount nationally calculated as modest but adequate in basic essentials.

• Until such time as a national minimum income is enacted by the Congress, the Commission recommends that the State of Ohio revise its minimum budget upward to the federally

---

[5]For a fuller discussion of children's allowances, see *Children's Allowances and the Economic Welfare of Children,* ed. by Eveline Burns, Citizens Committee for Children, New York, 1968.

established poverty line ($3,335 for a family of four, based on the 1968 cost of living). The Commission believes that no family in this state, eligible for assistance, should have to live below the poverty line.

HEALTH AND WELFARE LEVY

Voters of Cuyahoga County in May, 1968, passed a 3-mill levy for health and welfare, enabling the county to raise $18,400,000, an increase of $5,600,000 above the previous 2-mill levy's $12,800,000.

Recommendation

- The Commission strongly urges that, with due allowance for mandatory expenditures, more than half of the additional funds raised by the 3-mill levy should be used to increase payments for AFDC nearer to 100% of the Ohio minimum standard. Indeed, the County Board of Commissioners has assured the Commission that the "most significant" amount of the additional funds raised will be used for this purpose. This pledge should be honored.

STATE INCOME TAX

The inadequacy of welfare payments in Ohio is evident in the desperate condition of children eligible for Aid to Families with Dependent Children, who suffer malnutrition and endure indignities in the community. Even if the State Legislature would release funds to bring payments up to the minimum standards set by the state itself, destitution, disease, dependency, and a deteriorating environment still would be the lot of many welfare recipients.

We reiterate that budget standards and payments must be raised *substantially* at the state level to achieve even minimum levels of health and decency. And we want to emphasize that even minimum standards and payments will require additional taxation, which we are ready to support.

Any consideration of new taxes must give attention to their legal, political, and economic aspects. An examination needs to be made of the total structure of state and local taxes and the constitutional provisions governing specific tax legislation.

The tax to be enacted, its form and rates, must be equitable. In the final analysis, we as responsible citizens must support new taxes and tax increases when human needs demand public fulfillment.

Ohio is one of the richest states in the nation, but its tax revenue and welfare payments rank with the poorest states. By contemporary criteria, we have not taxed ourselves anywhere near our capacity.[6] The Advisory Commission on Intergovernmental Relations in its *Measures of State and Local Fiscal Capacity* in October, 1962, rated the tax efforts of Ohio as 41st, 43rd, and 42nd among the states on the basis of personal income, income produced, and composite income, respectively.

The need for increased state appropriations and an increase in state taxes is clear. Relying on the studies made by tax economists in Ohio, and by the Ohio Tax Study Commission (1966-67), the Mayor's Commission, after considerable deliberation, recommends that the state enact a tax on personal income and on the income of corporations. The majority of states are already using income taxes for needed revenue. At last count, 37 states and the District of Columbia levy taxes on personal income (24 of these states also have sales tax), and 38 states levy taxes on income of corporations.

State income taxes are equitable, since they adhere to the principle of ability to pay. Income is the best measure of tax-paying capacity, and taxes in almost all instances are ultimately paid out of income.

State income taxes are productive. To illustrate, a tax on personal income at an average effective rate of 1% would yield $270 million at the 1965 level of income in Ohio. A tax on income of corporations at the rate of 5%, which is the median rate of states levying this tax, would yield $225 million.[7] In 1968 the two income taxes would yield over $500 million.

---

[6]The Ohio Tax Study Commission *Staff Study*, 1966-67, compared Ohio with ten other industrial states (California, Illinois, Indiana, Massachusetts, Michigan, New Jersey, New York, Pennsylvania, Texas, and Wisconsin) in per capita public spending for 1964-65. For education, Ohio ranked tenth, for health and hospitals ninth, welfare eighth, highways sixth, all other public expenditures ninth. In all categories Ohio ranked below the national average.

[7]Ohio Tax Study Commission, *Staff Study*.

There are other sources of new tax revenue. An increase of 1% of the sales tax could bring $110 million annually. However, Ohio raised the sales tax from 3% to 4% in 1967. A further increase might introduce a significant degree of tax regression, but an increase in revenue from the sales tax is available in another way—through extending the tax to services such as automobile repair and maintenance, general repair, laundry and dry cleaning, barbering, beauty treatments, amusements, and advertisements. At the 4% rate, sales tax on services might bring $67 million.

A value-added tax or a gross-receipts tax has been proposed. These taxes on business activities, or turnover, have some characteristics which are similar to those of the sales tax, but with heightened regressiveness. These taxes do not differentiate between profitable and money-losing businesses, therefore their impact is unequal and their regression is serious. The only state which enacted the value-added tax, Michigan, repealed it and replaced it with a corporation income tax.

The state could raise the private automobile license fee from $10 to $20 and gain about $45 million. It could also raise the gasoline tax, but the revenue from these sources under present laws generally goes to finance highways and highway safety. The state in 1966–67 obtained $55 million from the cigarette tax (5 cents a pack) and earned about $80 million from liquor control. The tax on cigarettes and liquor profits could be raised. However, the increase yields would not amount to substantial sums.

A very substantial increase in state revenue is needed, for there are several areas of public services, such as education and mental health care, which, like welfare, are not adequately financed. Income taxes clearly appear to be the best and virtually the only adequate source of additional revenue. Revenue from income taxes will rise as the state's economy grows, permitting the state to provide expanded public services as time goes on. The fact that three-quarters of the states levy personal and corporation taxes attests to the need and desirability of such direct taxes. State income taxes are deductible for federal income tax purposes. This favorable provision in the federal revenue code must not go unused.

Contrary to some popular myths, low taxes do not necessarily aid economic growth. Some states with greater tax burdens have shown higher rates of economic growth than Ohio.

Careful research indicates that the tax level is no critical factor in industrial location decisions.[8] The Commission is of the opinion that for business and individuals alike the benefits from improved public services are likely to overbalance the added tax costs.

Taxes on personal and corporate income can also be levied by counties. However, there are vast fiscal disparities among Ohio's counties, and there is no reason to believe that variations in need match those in fiscal capacity. Ohio already goes further than most states in throwing local communities back on their resources to finance their public service needs. This trend can well be reversed.

Ohio can neither resolve the crisis in welfare nor provide adequate education, health, mental health, housing, youth employment, and other vital services while it remains in the bottom rank of states in proportion of income allocated to public services.

Recommendation

- The Commission supports the necessity for higher taxation in Ohio, especially at the state level. The Commission believes the state income tax is the fairest and most practical method of raising the necessary funds.

WELFARE ADMINISTRATION—ELIGIBILITY AND SERVICE

"Public assistance" suggests help, support and comfort to those in need. One should be able to assume that those seeking such aid or receiving assistance could expect help as a right and that the system and its administration would be oriented to offer and deliver help effectively and quickly.

---

[8] A *Business Week* survey conducted in 1958 showed that, in considering the factors in determining industrial location, businessmen mentioned market in 25% of their replies, labor in 18%, transportation facilities in 12%, availability in 11%, and taxes in 5%. The *Staff Study* of the Ohio Tax Study Commission stated that "the consensus of those who have studied the matter is that taxes are only a marginal consideration in the decision as to locating a business in one state or another" (Chapter 15, p. 20). It cited Henry L. Hunker and Alfred J. Wright, *Factors of Industrial Location in Ohio,* Ohio State University Press, Columbus, 1963.

Instead, welfare departments throughout the country often communicate suspicion of clientele and mete out punishment. Rather than quick, efficient service, delay is more often the rule. It is not a matter of hostile workers or administrators—but rather that such attitudes are fostered by the system.

The caseworker,[9] burdened by complex federal, state, and county eligibility procedures that must be followed to ensure reimbursement, becomes concerned first with paper, second with people.

A recent survey by the Cuyahoga County Welfare Department revealed *that 77% of the worker's time was spent on procedures and paperwork,* leaving almost no time for the problems of the client.

The general public tends to view welfare clients from a position of ignorance, apathy, and sometimes prejudice. When public demands that clients be treated as undeserving are reflected in legislation and regulations, the workers become both the agents and the victims of general public desire for strict controls. It is a tribute to many workers and supervisors that they exercise humanity and helpfulness despite, rather than because of, the way the welfare system operates.

Many of the existing regulations are not as liberally interpreted as they could be by the County Welfare Department because of state directives. For example:

The Federal Handbook of Public Assistance Administration, Section IV, 2200–2230, says: "Reliance on the applicant (and public records) as the primary source of information will ordinarily make it unnecessary to consult other sources of information. The agency should take no steps in the exploration of eligibility to which the applicant does not agree, including contact with collateral sources." An interpretation of eligibility would thus indicate that the client himself should be the main source of information to determine eligibility. It would follow that the burden of proof of ineligibility lies with the welfare department and the use of public records.

However, the Ohio State Department of Welfare interprets the federal policy of the client as "primary" source to mean

---

[9]Formerly (and more precisely) termed social investigators. They are usually untrained. Of the 270 social workers in public assistance in the Cuyahoga County Department of Welfare, for example, only four or five are professionally educated social workers. The supervisors usually are trained professionals with graduate degrees in social work.

that the client is merely the "first" source of information. The social worker, called upon to administer rigid regulations, often is seen by the client as an adversary. Under these circumstances even the most dedicated and sensitive of workers finds it difficult to be an advocate of the poor.

Social workers are overburdened by the sheer weight of work. Though federal and state regulations call for 60 families as a maximum caseload per worker, some caseloads are as high as 200. The average caseload in Cuyahoga County is 135. The shortage of caseworkers in Cuyahoga County means that approximately 1,700 cases, representing approximately 4,200 persons, have no worker assigned to them. Of an authorized staff of 499, the department has 109 vacancies, of which 25 are caseworker vacancies.

"Chances are," a County Welfare Department official told the Commission, "the caseworker is familiar with 10 of these [135 cases], has 5 that present constant problems, and the other 120 are merely statistics."

It is hard to be caring to a statistic. Indeed, the frustrations for workers who see and feel the problems of recipients and are unable to help, constitute a factor in the high turnover of personnel in the County Welfare Department. The annual turnover rate in 1967 was 57% among county caseworkers.

In the past, the Cuyahoga County Welfare Department has made financial contributions to individuals to attend graduate school. Some 54 have received such financial aid. Of 40 who completed graduate study and (as stipulated in the loan contract) returned to the Welfare Department to work, approximately 18 still remain.

The complex eligibility procedures make it difficult for a poor person to exercise his right to seek aid when it is needed. The Department of Health, Education, and Welfare indicates that for every person receiving public assistance aid, three persons are living with incomes below the poverty level but receiving no financial help. The reasons are many but a few stand out. Many states, for example, require that an indigent person reside in the state for at least a year before he is eligible to apply for financial aid. Though several federal courts have ruled this regulation unconstitutional, it continues to be enforced.

In Cuyahoga County, childless couples and single adults are not qualified for any type of assistance, unless they are blind, permanently disabled, or more than 65 years of age. Also, in a majority of states a family cannot qualify for aid unless the father is deceased, disabled, or out of the home. The last condition is a factor in the breakup of many low income families.

But the majority of the poor receive no aid simply because they have made no formal application. Some who seek help are discouraged by intake workers who have (or communicate) restrictive attitudes. Others are discouraged by intimidating questions. Many avoid application because of the stigma attached by society to those receiving welfare. It is a stigma that says one is less than human or has failed as a human being if help is accepted.

The lack of information available to the client leads to the charge that the welfare departments of the country serve to keep the poor from receiving aid. The contrast is made with the availability of information for veteran or Social Security benefits. Indeed, the massive federal government recruitment of eligible elderly people for the Medicare program sharply contrasts with the almost secretive attitude of the government in regard to eligibility for public assistance. The news media have not been used to inform those in need of available assistance. Probably the only attempt to provide adequate information to the poor about eligibility has been made by recipients themselves through the Welfare Rights Movement.

Those groups and individuals—neighborhood settlements, poverty centers, ministers—who have contact with the poor should be prime sources of information, but often they do not have the information or do not see it as part of their function. Even armed with adequate information, the poor have other hurdles before they can receive financial aid. The administrative procedures of application are themselves obstacles.

More efficient, more humane, and less costly methods of determining eligibility exist. Both business and government use random sampling effectively as a safeguard against possible losses resulting from fraud or honest mistakes.

Welfare departments, however, continue with the costly, inefficient, individual means test via a point-by-point investigation of all information the client gives, including income sources, family relationships, and other personal information the department deems pertinent. It is this time-consuming, tension-producing procedure that makes the social worker a clerk for most of the day rather than a professional giving needed service.

Despite the strict eligibility test, some 50% of the applicants to the Cuyahoga County Welfare Department do receive some form of emergency aid at the time of application—food stamps or payment of utilities. Indeed, 95% of applicants receive general relief assistance before eligibility is determined. This is a result partly of the lack of staff and partly of a more humane policy in dealing with applicant emergencies. But after an application has been approved, the probing process reappears as part of the continuing machinery to assess eligibility. For general relief clients, cases are reviewed every three months and for other categories, semiannual reviews are made. Thus, during the time the social worker and client should be developing understanding and trust, the checking and rechecking of eligibility fosters a feeling that both worker and client are natural antagonists.

To overcome this serious problem, a shift in emphasis is necessary from the presumption that a client is not eligible to one that presumes the applicant is eligible because he is truthful in his statements about need. This approach would make the administration of welfare properly client-centered. The client would be able to regard assistance as a matter of right, not charity. The worker could become more of a truly helping person. The burden of proof of ineligibility could be shifted from the client-applicant to the Welfare Department.

This same concept should be utilized in subsequent dealings. Welfare clients are supposed to have the right to have a number of emergency needs met. Beds, refrigerators, or other necessary household furniture are presumably available to meet such emergencies. However, the Welfare Department has no written definition of what an emergency is. Is it an emergency when a family has had utility service denied and the home has no heat in winter? Or if a client doesn't have a refrigerator and must preserve food and drink for the family? Or if the client's relief check has not been delivered or has been stolen?

These items are considered "exceptional" to the normal budgeted monthly allowance. Since they add to the costs of the welfare department, there is implicit and sometimes overt pressure to keep such requests minimal. These cases require the caseworker to use subjective judgment and thus exercise more power than is sound for either client or worker.

With respect to exceptional and emergency needs, as with eligibility, clients are not given adequate information about entitlements. Indeed, some of the social workers are unaware of the fundamental rights of the clients in these and other areas. Regulations, kept in a thick and expanding *State Welfare Manual,* are constantly in process of revision and most workers themselves cannot maintain a working knowledge of the rules. Supervisors are informed of major changes in the manual and are expected to advise caseworkers who do not have copies of the manual. Clients, of course, do not have easy access to the manual. Ironically, in the language of the present manual, access would be rather meaningless, since the manual puzzles even experienced lawyers.

Under such a complex, inflexible system—and one that operates at far less than the state itself considers bare subsistence levels—some safety mechanisms are necessary if justice and equity are to be approached. Yet, even where safety features exist, they operate poorly. The system, supposedly designed to create independence, fosters debilitating dependency.

Administrators of welfare have given the proponents of client rights, such as the client leaders of the Welfare Rights Movement, no recognition in the process of formulating policy or procedures. The process of fair hearings—by which clients appeal certain decisions that have been unfavorably ruled upon by the administration—is in need of correction. An equitable fair hearing process requires correction of several deficiencies, which include unreasonable delay of decision, no retroactive clause if the appeal is successful, lack of information as to the reason for denial, and lack of an impartial judge.

Although there is a Cuyahoga County Welfare Advisory Board, it has been moribund. No clients have been represented in the composition of this Board. The Board met only once during 1967—a period during which welfare rights were a crucial issue.

There has been some progress in the Cuyahoga County Welfare Department during the past few years, but basically the system under which it operates—defective on a national scale but especially restrictive as defined by the State of Ohio—is outmoded and inefficient, fostering both indignity and dependency. The recommendations which follow are designed to upgrade and reform the operation and to minimize its weaknesses until such time as a guaranteed annual income comes into being and the system in its present form can be dismantled.

Simplified Eligibility—Declaration of Income and Audit.

The present process for determining eligibility is expensive, time-consuming, and often humiliating to the client. The 77% of the workers' time spent in investigations of clients' eligibility status leaves almost no time for rendering social services.

The process could be simplified. At present the federal government permits the state to develop its own eligibility criteria and procedures for determining such eligibility.

The presumption of dishonesty on the part of applicants for public assistance is one of the major factors in promoting tension between dependent persons and the County Welfare Department and in contributing to the inefficiency of the Department. This presumption of dishonesty requires the applicant to *prove* his need by a stigmatizing means test.

Recommendations

• The County Commissioners should immediately seek state approval for the establishment of a procedure by which the client's declaration of income would be sufficient for determining eligibility. Such a plan would then be presented to the U.S. Department of Health, Education, and Welfare for final approval and should be followed by prompt and effective implementation.

• Initial applicants should establish eligibility by personal statements or affidavits relating to their financial situation and family composition.

• Following the initial establishment of eligibility, a sampling or "quality control" procedure should be instituted. Under this policy, the current eligibility practices would be carried out with a small sample of cases. This would apply both to initial eligibility and eligibility reviews.

Separation of Services and Income Payments. The current system of linking social services and eligibility determination is detrimental to the best interest of clients. Many social services are essential, but at present a client is compelled to accept "service" as a precondition for receiving income. This approach fosters an atmosphere of suspicion and distrust between workers and clients and reduces the potential effectiveness of social services to those clients who want and need them.

Many clients are capable of making arrangements for personal and family services from public and private institutions without the intervention of a "worker." This self-help role would provide for a greater sense of independence and security on the part of the recipient, as well as more rapid service.

Recommendations

- The Commission recommends that the procedures related to income maintenance be entirely separated from the delivery of social services. Services should be provided only on request except where services are of a protective nature.
- The provision of social services also should be made available upon request to those persons who do not meet eligibility requirements and are not recipients of public assistance.

Authorization at the County Level. A major complaint of welfare recipients and many caseworkers is the time-consuming and cumbersome procedures for special authorization at the state level, including special, medical, and dental services, medical appliances, and other items and/or services which require expenditures over and beyond the family budget.

Recommendations

- The state should utilize techniques of advanced management so that checks are delivered on time on a regular date.
- Authority should be given to the County Welfare Department to handle any emergency authorizations and to issue checks for such purposes at the local level.
- The timing of checks should be coordinated with the timing of food stamps.
- A local medical board should be authorized by the state to review and decide on all medical and dental requests, in lieu of decisions now made in Columbus, Ohio.

Liberalizing Eligibility Criteria. The present eligibility criteria throughout Ohio—and in Cuyahoga County—exclude large numbers of people who are in serious financial need.

Recommendations

- The Cuyahoga County Department of Welfare should revise its policies of eligibility so as to include all persons who fall under the income criteria and are not otherwise excluded by federal or state law.
- Where state policy is more restrictive than federal law in regard to eligibility, as in the case of residency requirements, state policy should be immediately liberalized.

- The General Relief program should be placed on a parity with other relief programs in relation to administrative criteria, eligibility requirements, and financing formula.

Client-Centered Administration. The administration of welfare services should be client-centered. This would require a major overhaul in the attitudes, training, and orientation of workers. Commitment and action on the part of policy-making officials are necessary to make this fundamental change in policy.[10]

Recommendations

- The burden of proof for denial of services should fall on the worker and agency rather than on the client as a matter of policy. The client should be thoroughly apprised of the reasons for denial of income or other services.
- The County Welfare Department should bear the costs of delay when clients appeal decisions related to eligibility or other client concerns. Clients should not suffer loss of income due to procedural delays.

THE NEED FOR A SIMPLIFIED MANUAL

Recipients of public welfare often do not receive services to which they are entitled simply because they do not know their rights. The State Department of Public Welfare issues a total of 2,000 copies of a manual spelling out the policies and regulations governing public assistance programs in the state. The Cuyahoga County Welfare Department receives 200 copies, which are issued to administrators, supervisors, and other key personnel. Caseworkers do not receive manuals and must receive interpretations from the supervisory staff. This creates inefficiency in client services because workers cannot always give appropriate and immediate interpretations to clients. Clients have no access to information concerning policies, other than the interpretation given by the workers.

The complexity and ambiguity of the manual dealing with policies and regulations of the County Welfare Department are major obstacles to meeting the financial and service needs of clients. The language of the manual is cumbersome and open

---

[10]See Appendix J for a discussion of presumptive eligibility.

to conflicting interpretations. The decisions regarding clothing, furniture, and appliances are arbitrary. Caseworkers and clients often have no clear understanding of the clients' rights and the agency's legal responsibilities because manuals are not available to the workers.

Recommendations

• The State Department of Public Welfare should develop a clear and complete manual which defines the rights and responsibilities of the clients and the agency. This manual should be readily available to all clients, workers, and community people dealing with problems of welfare. A special effort should be made by the County Welfare Department to have staff available at all times to interpret the manual for clients and interested persons.

• The Commission recommends that the State Department of Public Welfare develop a simplified handbook, based on the manual, outlining clearly and simply clients' rights, entitlements, and responsibilities and agency procedures. The handbook should be updated as necessary and made available to clients and all other interested citizens. For example, some facts that should be immediately interpreted to clients relate to the new work incentive provisions of the 1968 Social Security Amendments. Under these amendments, clients who work are allowed to keep the first $30 of their earned income plus one-third of the remainder.

FAIR HEARINGS FOR WELFARE CLIENTS

At present, fair hearings are provided only for the federally financed categories of relief, and hearing officers have interpreted this strictly so as to exclude consideration of general relief.

All states are required by the terms of the Social Security Act to provide recipients with an opportunity for a hearing in which they may contest adverse determinations. Throughout the Act can be found guarantees to recipients that their rights will not be affected by arbitrary administrative action, but the hearing practice in Cuyahoga County meets the standards of neither the federal government nor the Ohio Constitution.

A requirement in *The Federal Handbook of Public Assistance*

Administration states that every claimant be informed, in writing, at the time of application and at the time of any agency action affecting his claim, of his right to a fair hearing and of the method by which he may obtain a hearing. Ohio does print information about the opportunity for a hearing in a pamphlet that is distributed to caseworkers, but this is never distributed to clients. The County Welfare Department gives notice of the fair hearing right, but this is only *pro forma* in conformity with the requirement. As a practical matter, the poorly educated, unsophisticated welfare applicant deserves a more realistic oral explanation, buttressed by a separate pamphlet that would set out simply all of the procedural rights of clients. It should be spelled out that the client has the right to have a lawyer from the local legal aid society appeal his case in the event he is not satisfied with decisions.

Time for Decision. The right to a hearing is an empty right unless it includes the right to a decision within a reasonable time. The federal regulations recognize this in requiring a "prompt" determination and a state-set over-all time on decisions. In Ohio, the requirement is for a hearing and decision within 60 days of a request.

A review of fair hearings handled by the Legal Aid Society of Cleveland shows that, in some cases, as many as seven months elapse between the request for a hearing and the holding of the hearing. During this period of time the client is deprived of benefits, and even if the decision is ultimately in favor of the client, benefits are not often granted retroactively. Obviously this procedure inflicts extreme hardship on many clients who may be deprived of all benefits or a portion of their entitlements between the time of the adverse agency action and the fair hearing decision.

The Right to a Prior Hearing. Denial of the right to a prompt hearing would not be so disastrous if Cuyahoga County did not also deny clients their right to a hearing *before* an adverse agency action takes effect. Due process usually requires that a hearing be held in an administrative proceeding before the final order becomes effective. This suggests that clients should have reasonable *notice* of the agency's intention to seriously reduce or withdraw assistance and the right to prompt appeal prior to the action contemplated. Otherwise such reduction or withdrawal should be stayed pending appeal by the client (as is the case in other areas of law).

Reasons for Denial. A fair hearing held before or after adverse agency action is of little value to the client who does not know why he has been cut off or denied assistance. Federal regulations require that the notice of adverse action must contain the reason why and must provide a basis for the individual to express dissatisfaction with the agency action. Only then can he know whether he has a legitimate grievance, and only then can he prepare his case for a hearing. This means that in an adverse action the client should be *informed* of the specific rule or policy for the adverse action and the facts justifying the action.

Hearing Procedures and Judicial Review. Hearing procedures do not currently meet the requirements of due process, nor can the procedures be considered fair hearings because procedures and appeals from hearings are vested in officials of the County Welfare Department. Since the Department's own interests may be at stake, judgment should be taken out of the hands of the Department and lodged with *impartial* arbiters. Independent bodies of referees and arbiters should be established to hear and decide welfare appeal—possibly through the cooperation of an arbitration association or the local bar association. In addition, the Ohio Administrative Procedure Act should be amended to provide for appeals from welfare hearings to the courts. Just as judicial review is provided in the case of numerous other state-administered hearings, it should be provided in the case of public welfare hearings.

The confidential nature of welfare records should be understood primarily as protection for the client, not the agency. This is particularly important in view of the fact that workers involved in the original decision upon which the complaint is based are often not available to testify. Consequently, testimony is provided by the current worker assigned to the case, who must refer to the case record. The case record should be similarly available to the client's attorney. Lacking access to the case record, the client cannot adequately be represented by his attorney.

Procedures in Fraud Accusations. One area that must be

certified is that of the right to due process and fair hearing in cases involving accusation of fraud, illicit income, and improper conduct. The traditional practice of vesting, to a large extent, the power of decision in the hands of the welfare administration, however objective, helps maintain a custodial relationship and a climate of submissiveness.

Recommendations

- Fair hearings should be immediately extended to cover cases of General Relief.
- At the time of application, clients should be orally informed of their right to a fair hearing, and this right should also be clearly and unequivocably set forth in a "clients' rights manual."
- When there is a reason for denial, clients should be informed of the specific reason.
- The County Welfare Department should bear the costs of delay when clients have appealed decisions related to eligibility or other client concerns. Clients should not suffer loss of income due to procedural delays.
- Fair hearings should be held before impartial referees or arbiters outside the welfare system. The Ohio Administrative Procedure Act should be amended to provide for judicial review of fair hearings.
- The client's advocate in the fair hearing should have access to all materials pertinent to the decision.
- In cases related to fraud, an informal meeting should be held, involving the caseworker, the client, and the supervisor, at which the charges are presented and discussed and the client given the opportunity to discuss their validity. The client should be informed of his right to representation and the availability of legal aid services.

DECENTRALIZATION OF SERVICES

Geographic decentralization of the Cuyahoga County Welfare Department is needed, and currently the Department is moving toward geographic decentralization by opening five neighborhood offices to provide: (1) intake service, (2) emergency relief assistance, (3) telephone contact with central office for clients, (4) food stamp certification, (5) expediter services (emergency), and (6) a housing program.

Persons with financial need should be able to receive immediate aid at the local office. Caseworkers should be more accessible. Operational contacts with clients should provide the agency with insights in neighborhood and client problems—insights that are lacking under a central structure. The experiences of local office personnel should be utilized as a basis for planning and policy development at the central structure level.

Recommendation
- The County Welfare Department should decentralize its administration to provide for intake, supervision, casework, and other supportive services at the neighborhood level. The central administrative unit should be primarily concerned with planning, policy-making, coordination of services, administration of payments, and research and evaluation.

COUNTY WELFARE ADVISORY BOARD

The County Welfare Advisory Board has been allowed to become an unrepresentative, moribund body, which does not meet regularly and performs no significant functions. The Board consists of five to nine members with responsibility for recommending policies, programs, and regulations. Its members were appointed prior to January 1, 1967, and one member by law must be a juvenile court judge or his designee. It met once in 1967. In no sense is this panel advisory at the present time, nor has it historically played a significant role in welfare policy. A genuine advisory body can be extremely effective in increasing the communication between the Director of the County Welfare Department and various segments of the community.

Recommendation
- The County Welfare Advisory Board should be reactivated so as to take part in the formulation of policies and programs. It should make recommendations to the Director of the County Welfare Department and the County Commissioners. It should meet bimonthly, at the minimum, or at the request of Board members. Client organizations and the city administration should be represented. The Board should have available the information and records of the County Welfare Department and should receive complete Department assistance in its studies, evaluations, and recommendations.

STATE WELFARE ADVISORY BOARD

The State of Ohio makes minimal provisions for citizen involvement in policy-making for vital health and welfare services, representing major expenditures of tax dollars and touching the lives of a significant number of people. Other states, particularly New York, rely on citizen commissions and boards to assist in state welfare policy formulations. A citizen advisory board could provide valuable services to the State Department of Public Welfare and to state officials and administrators in interpreting the concerns of citizens in the local communities.

At the state level, delays in authorization for services to clients have created numerous problems, including late checks and inefficient handling of requests. A State Welfare Advisory Board could provide insight for improving current methods of providing services at the state level. Such a board should give immediate attention to the delays in authorizations to local welfare agencies for services to clients.

Recommendation

- The State Department of Public Welfare should seek authority as soon as possible from the Ohio Legislature to establish a State Welfare Advisory Board, representing a broad spectrum of the citizenry. Representation from client organizations and the large urban counties and cities should be mandatory.

CITY REPRESENTATIVE FOR WELFARE

Although the City of Cleveland has no direct responsibility for the administration of public welfare programs, the majority of the 87,786 recipients of public assistance (as of December 31, 1967) in Cuyahoga County resided within the city. About 31,000 families whose income is less than $3,000 annually resided in the depressed areas of Cleveland, according to 1965 figures. About 2,000 of these families had incomes of less than $2,000 per year.

The city should have an official who would represent the interests of the welfare population in Cleveland with respect to education, health, employment, and job training. His responsibilities would include serving on the County Welfare Advisory Board, being available to welfare clientele for redress of grievances when other avenues have failed, having authoritative knowledge of the local welfare situation, being involved in the planning of decentralized welfare centers, and serving as liaison with voluntary agencies.

Recommendation

* The Mayor should appoint an official, possibly within the proposed Department of Economic Development and Human Resources, to represent the interests of the welfare population of the City of Cleveland with the city services, with the County Welfare Department, and with the private sector.

SOCIAL SECURITY AMENDMENTS OF 1967

The original intent of public assistance programs within the Social Security Act was to provide financial assistance and social services to strengthen and maintain family life in time of need.

Though the 1967 Amendments of the Social Security Act provide some increased services and liberalized practices—including training programs, some help to unemployed fathers, and needed day care facilities for working mothers—the general nature of the Amendments subverts the original concept by coercive and restrictive elements, reflecting a dangerously punitive mood within Congress and throughout the nation toward the poor.[11]

The legislation has limitations that the Mayor's Commission views as hazardous for the following reasons: (1) It limits self-determination on the part of the mother who wants to care for her child. (2) It makes possible punitive judgments by requiring staff to determine who is "appropriate" for employment. (3) It freezes AFDC funds, a move that could lead to many families in need receiving no aid and could have the effect of lowering present meager payments. (4) It allows welfare departments to expand the use of vendor payments rather than cash, a move that will increase dependency, rather than encourage self-sufficiency. (5) It limits help for unemployed fathers by requiring the father to have had six or more quarters of employment in any 13-quarter period before application.

Recommendations

* The Social Security Amendments of 1967 should be changed

---

[11]See Appendix P for a more detailed account of the provisions of the 1967 Amendments affecting the public welfare program.

to delete the coercive features which force AFDC mothers to accept employment. Recipients should have the same options as other mothers to determine their roles in relation to their families.
• The Department of Labor and the Department of Health, Education, and Welfare should provide for periodic inspection and evaluation of training programs, employment situations, and day care centers to determine the effectiveness of these programs and prevent exploitation of recipients.
• The AFDC program for unemployed fathers should be mandatory in all states and steps should be taken to apply for AFDC on the basis of need rather than on the basis of quarters worked under Social Security Act provisions.
• The principle of cash payments under public assistance should be strengthened by curtailment of the Protective Payments provision. In all cases where states use the present provisions, they should be required to "show cause." The Regional Office of the Department of Health, Education, and Welfare should approve of each such arrangement on an individual basis, using the criterion that the best interest of the family will be served. Payments should be administered in such a way as to preserve maximum dignity and self-direction of recipients. All affected clients should be clearly informed as to their right to appeal such a decision.
• The amendment in the 1967 Amendments "freezing" the number of children under AFDC should be repealed immediately.

A BILL OF RIGHTS FOR WELFARE CLIENTS— A GENERAL STATEMENT OF THE COMMISSION

No person should be denied his rights or privileges as a citizen by virtue of a condition of poverty or dependency on public welfare. We affirm the following as basic rights and privileges in a free society:

Right to Public Assistance. All citizens who find themselves in a condition of economic and/or social dependency have a right to public assistance under the prevailing welfare system. Assistance should be provided at an income level adequate to meet the needs of the recipient.

Right to Assistance and Services with Respect and Dignity. All persons eligible for public assistance have a right to receive financial aid with full respect for the dignity and privacy of the individual. They are also entitled to full use of public services in the community—such as health, housing, education, and library services—and these services should be provided with the same courtesy to the needy as to any other citizen and they should provide the same benefits.

Right to Decent Housing and Environment. Welfare recipients are entitled to live in housing and in neighborhoods that are decent, safe, sanitary, and suitable to family requirements.

Right to Equal Employment Opportunity. Welfare recipients should have equal opportunity, if physically and mentally able, to be gainfully employed in jobs which provide income adequate to individual and family needs. Mothers, who are clients, have the right, as do other citizens, to decide whether to seek training and employment or to devote themselves to the needs of their families.

Right to Health Services. Welfare recipients have a right to quality professional care to meet their medical, dental, and pharmaceutical needs. Professional services should be provided with dignity and should be commensurate with services provided for the general public.

Right to Quality Education. Children who are recipients of public assistance have a right to educational experiences equal to those provided in the better school systems in the community. The educational experience should be related to preparing such recipients and other low-income children for meaningful participation in the economic and social life of the nation.

Right to Equal Protection of the Law. Welfare recipients must be afforded their constitutional rights to due process and equal protection of the law. These rights include the right to, and availability of, free legal counsel in dealings with government officials and in matters before the courts. Clients have the right to clear and impartial publicized procedures for the resolution of grievances and to equity of treatment by courts, welfare administrators, police, and other public officials. They have a right to adequate police protection and to the enforcement of laws, supported by necessary personnel and procedures.

Right to Advocacy. The public assistance recipient has a right to act as an advocate in his own behalf and to participate as a free citizen in social and political action activities without institutional harassment; he has a right to expect that institutions will be so designed as to assist the poor with this conviction; the recipient has the same right as other constituent groups to participate in institutional and political decision-making which affects his life and welfare.

All of the foregoing are based on the premise of the right of welfare recipients to life. They have the right to expect that the citizenry, social institutions, and representatives of government will be concerned with the degrading conditions which affect the lives of the impoverished. High mortality rates, crippling diseases, malnutrition, and gross handicaps resulting from institutional inadequacies, social exclusion, and poor environments have created a population with a declining ability to participate in the social and economic life of the nation. Denial of resources necessary to reverse the trends of human despair and hopelessness suggests that society must be reminded of the individual's simple right to survive.

3. EMPLOYMENT AND TRAINING

To much of the public, the obvious solution to public welfare is employment. This is an illusion. As stressed in our initial chapter, it is the least likely solution for those now receiving relief and for many other poor. Most people on public welfare simply cannot be employed.

Yet, in the long-term view, employment must be regarded as the chief means of breaking the dependency cycle now perpetuated by the welfare system. Indeed, for the largest group receiving support—the children of welfare families—the prospect of employment and the availability of relevant training programs should provide incentives for self-sufficiency.

Appropriate measures also are required to enable men to have the opportunities to enter the economic mainstream through employment. This means that the federal government must be the employer of last resort. Stable family life depends upon the ability of low-income males to earn enough to marry and support a family on a level of decency.

The Mayor's Commission on the Crisis in Welfare sees child care and household operation as a full-time job for mothers who wish to devote their time to their young children in a welfare family. In addition, it insists that appropriate and well-supported employment and training programs should be available to those mothers wishing work or desiring to prepare themselves for the labor market at a future date. Special attention also should be given to employing and utilizing the talents of blind and partially disabled persons who desire employment, and to breaking down the barriers of discrimination and apathy in meeting their needs.

Most people, including most of those receiving public assistance, would prefer employment to idleness if they had the choice, if for no other reason than that our national ethic equates work with worth and self-esteem.

Employment opportunities presently afford most individuals the ability to maximize their earning power—but not all. In a statistical work force of some 920,000 in Greater Cleveland only some 24,000, or about 2.4%, are reported as unemployed, compared with 3.7% for the nation, but these figures are misleading, and in Cleveland, the estimate of jobless persons in depressed areas goes as high as 40,000.[1] Thousands of individuals for many reasons elude the normal statistical measurements of unemployment. Realizing this, the U.S. Department of Labor used other methods to determine unemployment in depressed areas in 1967. The results showed that in Cleveland's depressed areas—Glenville, Hough, Central, Kinsman, and the Near West Side—15.5% were unemployed.[2] The unemployment rate had increased from 13.7% in 1960. In addition, another 14.7% were not counted as unemployed, because lack of success in the job market had so depressed them that they had given up seeking work.

Unemployment in depressed areas strikes at all segments of the population, women and young adults, as well as the male work force.

For example, a survey of the out-of-school youth by the Cleveland public schools in 1966 revealed that 47% of the youth aged 16 to 21 were unemployed in the 12 inner-city areas covered.[3] In some areas the problem was more severe: in East Central, it was 65%; in Hough, 60%; and in Central, 58%. The survey revealed that it made little difference if the individuals had graduated from high school or had had further job training. Approximately half the unemployed youth were high school graduates, and for those who participated in job training programs the unemployment rate was about the same (54%). In 1967 a U.S. Department of Labor report showed 58% of out-of-school youth were unemployed in the same areas.

Despite the fact that Negro women in urban poverty areas hold more jobs than white women generally—43.6% to 36.5% —unemployment works a heavy burden on mothers receiving

---

[1] *Area Trends in Employment and Unemployment,* U.S. Department of Labor, Manpower Administration, December, 1967.

[2] *Subemployment in the City of Cleveland,* Survey of the U.S. Department of Labor, December, 1967.

[3] *Unemployed Out-of-School Youth Survey,* Cleveland Public Schools, 1966.

public assistance, many of them Negro. The County Welfare Department estimates that 13,100 mothers are receiving public assistance. Many would rather work but are blocked from the labor market for various reasons, including discrimination by race and sex, lack of skills and education, poor health, and family responsibilities. Even most of the available training programs do not relate to the needs of females.

Getting a job does not always provide much of an answer to those living in depressed areas. Often the jobs pay little. For example, one of every two Negroes in the inner city are subemployed—earning less than $60 per week as a head of a household for full-time employment and less than $56 per week as a single individual.[4]

Racial discrimination, past and present, has restricted the Negro to the less secure, less desirable, and less rewarding jobs in our society. Discrimination has caused and reinforced extreme hopelessness and frustration in the lives of many now receiving public assistance. Its legacy of despair has not only deprived them of the necessary skills to benefit from some opening opportunities but remains a potent reason for apathy.

Restrictions upon Negroes become evident by the fact that nearly one-third of all employed urban Negroes are in service occupations and one-tenth in private households.[5] Of employed Negro women, 56% hold menial service jobs, of which half are in private households. The largest proportion of Negro men work as operatives or laborers, jobs of diminishing significance in our modern technological economy.

Laws to enforce equal opportunities in the labor force are at best underenforced by federal and state enforcement agencies, which are woefully understaffed. Both industry and unions have far to go to eliminate blatant discrimination. Only with great public pressure were 43 nonwhite apprenticeships opened in 1967 in the five major construction craft unions in Cleveland. Although this is hailed as a major breakthrough, in reality it is still tokenism, and all too prevalent in labor and management.

Though attempts at training and retraining programs are being made, they are expensive and limited, and results are

---

[4] *Subemployment in the City of Cleveland.*

[5] *Poverty Areas of Major Cities,* U.S. Department of Labor, Manpower Division, Special Labor Force Report No. 75, December, 1965.

often frustrating. The 22 Special Manpower Training Programs in Cleveland provided services to 8,000 persons during the first six months of 1967.[6] The estimated number of placements of the 22 programs was 2,500, or about 30% of the original enrollees. The dropout rate by program ranged from 10% to 36%. Some 80% were high school dropouts. The 30% placement record diminishes even more when one considers the type of jobs involved—primarily jobs in the unskilled, semiskilled, and service areas in medium and small industries. More than half were jobs as machine operators, in hospital occupations, and in office services.

The trend to locate plants away from the city, combined with strong housing discrimination in the suburbs and poor public transportation, present additional obstacles to those trapped in depressed areas. In the past, when low skills were more in demand, housing for workers surrounded factory sites.

A vivid illustration of the transportation problems was provided by the Watts district of Los Angeles, an area severely handicapped by lack of public transportation. Not until the district erupted in rioting did the public show concern for the problem. Subsequently, bus service was created with federal financial assistance, and within two months the line was carrying 10,000 passengers weekly. A survey showed that most of the passengers were either going to work or seeking employment.

Rationale and statistics to supplement and explain each of the following recommendations for employment and training will be found in Appendix O under the appropriate heading.

JOB TRAINING, EMPLOYMENT STANDARDS, AND ENTRY-PAY LEVELS

Recommendations

- The Manpower Training Programs should provide training and job placement for adults for those occupations which pay at, or above, the national minimum wage scale.
- The Mayor should encourage the National Alliance of Businessmen, the Greater Cleveland Growth Association, and the trade unions to evaluate and change entry-level job require-

---

[6]*The Manpower Planning and Development Commission of the Welfare Federation of Cleveland,* September, 1967.

ments wherever feasible in order to open job opportunities for the unemployed.

RACIAL DISCRIMINATION IN EMPLOYMENT AND IN CRAFT UNIONS

Recommendations

• The city administration should request state legislation to provide for additional funds to increase the staff of the Ohio Civil Rights Commission. In addition, there should be legislation which strengthens the Civil Rights Commission's authority to launch investigations of discrimination where there is evidence of racial bias and when formal complaint has not been lodged with the Commission.

• The U.S. Department of Labor and the U.S. Equal Employment Opportunity Commission should increase the compliance program staff in the Greater Cleveland area.

COMMUNITY SERVICE EMPLOYMENT PROJECTS FOR THE UNEMPLOYED

Recommendation

• As a first priority in 1969 the Congress should enact legislation to provide for a national program of community service employment, financed by the federal government and administered by private industry and local governments. In these programs industry would be reimbursed for special costs of training and placement. Where industry could not offer the positions, local governments would organize the community service projects as the employer of last resort. These positions should be important to the employee and to the community and be compensated, at least, at federal minimum wage levels.

DEVELOPMENT OF INDUSTRY IN DEPRESSED AREAS

Recommendations

• The Greater Cleveland Growth Association, in cooperation with the City of Cleveland, should develop and promote more vigorously an immediate program to utilize vacant inner-city

land to attract, retain, and expand job-producing businesses and industries. These industries should be adapted to the ecology of the area and meet code requirements of the City of Cleveland.
• The City of Cleveland should expand its efforts to provide low-cost land, free utilities, and other incentives as an inducement for business and industry to locate in the inner city.

TRANSPORTATION

Recommendations

• The Cleveland Transit System should apply for a grant from the federal government to demonstrate the feasibility and importance of providing direct transportation from the inner city to major industrial parks.
• Major employers on the outskirts of the city should be encouraged by the National Alliance of Businessmen to develop their own transportation system to the inner city or key transit stops. This service would be of value to persons having great difficulty in reaching job sites.
• In the event the Transit Company is unable to attract demonstration money, a public subsidy should be created from local tax money to help support the plan for increased services of public transportation to enable workers in depressed areas to reach their work sites. This type of public support would make it feasible either to lower transit fares or keep fares within the reach of low-income groups.

EMPLOYMENT OF WOMEN

Recommendations

• The Special Manpower Training Programs should make a special effort to recruit and train women from poverty areas for clerical positions in cooperation with the adult education program of the Cleveland public schools.
• The National Alliance of Businessmen, in their opening of job slots for the chronically unemployed, should recruit and place women with cooperating industries in clerical or industrial jobs through on-the-job training.

EMPLOYMENT OF AFDC MOTHERS

Recommendations

- The Ohio Department of Employment Security and the Ohio Department of Public Welfare should establish regulations designed to protect the rights of AFDC mothers who will be affected by the work provisions of the Social Security Amendments of 1967. These regulations should ensure protection in the process of selecting mothers for training and jobs, in the nature of training and employment, hours of work, salaries, and child care. They should ensure the right of AFDC mothers to protection by other provisions which currently relate to the protection of women in employment situations.
- The New Careers for the Poor program is demonstrating that employable clients can be trained for subprofessional occupations in day care centers, social service agencies, hospitals, and schools. The Commission recommends that planning be initiated to expand training and employment opportunities for welfare clients as subprofessionals in human service occupations.

DAY CARE FACILITIES FOR WORKING MOTHERS

Recommendations

- The Mayor and the County Commissioners should call upon private employers to urge the development of day care centers immediately. Business, industry, labor, and voluntary organizations should develop centers at work sites or other appropriate places where there are large groups of employed mothers. These centers would not be used exclusively by trainees and employees who are members of a client group but would be for the utilization of all employees. This expansion and creation of day care centers should be done in cooperation with the local effort for AFDC mothers in day care planning.
- In addition, the city should establish and assist in operating day care facilities developed in neighborhoods at training sites, work sites, and wherever else feasible.
- All day care facilities should have appropriate staff structure for supervision and direction of services.
- A state code of regulations should be developed to provide for licensing of all day care facilities and provision of consistent and adequate care.

- The City of Cleveland should immediately revise the section of the city code related to day care services for children. The new code should reflect regulations commensurate with accepted professional standards.

SERVICE INDUSTRY EMPLOYMENT PROGRAM

Recommendation

- The City of Cleveland should undertake, with federal funds, the establishment of a job placement program providing for contractual arrangements with the private employment sector. This program would provide jobs for persons seeking full-time or part-time service-related employment. The city or the contracting employment agencies would be responsible for placing unemployed and low-income residents in jobs offered by small employers. These jobs would have to meet appropriate standards related to wages, hours, and general working conditions.

YOUTH EMPLOYMENT

Recommendations

- In order to meet the special employment needs of all poverty youth, including AFDC youth, unemployed high school dropouts, and youth not eligible for welfare assistance, the Commission urges that the Mayor, the U.S. Office of Economic Opportunity, and the business community should strive for additional state and federal funds and maximum business community support so that enrollment in all programs can be expanded to serve all eligible youth. The business community must be urged to provide suitable openings for the youth that are trained.
- The County Welfare Department, the Cleveland Board of Education, and the Probation Department of Juvenile Court should aid in this expanded effort by immediately developing a listing of all eligible youth. These lists should be forwarded to the Mayor's Council on Youth Opportunity in order to recruit and contact those in need of employment and to coordinate the various employment efforts. All potential links to the youth community should be utilized to supplement this effort.
- The Mayor's Council on Youth Opportunity should develop

an ongoing program to secure part-time employment for poverty youth *throughout the school year.*

FOLLOW-UP AND SUPPORTIVE SERVICES FOR SPECIAL MANPOWER PROGRAMS

Recommendation

• The proposed Department of Human and Economic Resources of the City of Cleveland, in cooperation with the Special Manpower Programs, should make an immediate request to the U.S. Department of Labor for funds to provide for an adequate number of staff for counseling and service follow-up on pre-employment training, training program dropouts, potential enrollees lost during referral, and persons placed in employment. Funds should also be increased to extend the periods of time allocated for job orientation and remedial programs. The feasibility of coordinating the counseling service under a single auspice for all training programs should be considered as one means of providing an efficient and effective service.

4. EDUCATION

In an age when viable careers are tied increasingly to technological skills, effective education becomes a major vehicle for breaking the poverty-welfare cycle and enabling the poor to enter the economic mainstream of American life. Thus, the Cleveland public schools are strategic to an all-out attack on the problems of welfare and poverty.

Unfortunately, a number of major obstacles prevent the Cleveland schools from effectively functioning in this role. Not the least is the lack of adequate financing and the educational flaws caused by this shortage. Despite increased expenditure and extra state and federal funds amounting to $100 a child, expenditures per child in the city are only about 80% of the expenditure in the average Cleveland suburb, which has 20% smaller classes.

The inability of a teacher to give educationally disadvantaged children adequate help in a class of sometimes as many as 40 children results in a continuation of poor learning achievement. Remedial programs often are unavailable in upper primary grades. New curricula, proper textbooks (especially with an interracial makeup), and even ordinary supplies regarded as minimum in suburban schools are lacking because of fund shortages.

In its school foundation law for allocating funds for school districts, the State of Ohio shortchanges Cleveland schools. This condition is the result of the state's failure to take into account the fact that municipal and county taxes in Cleveland amount to some 56% of the local tax dollar, while, in portions of Ohio outside major cities, municipal and county taxes account for only 32%.

The Ohio Legislature in 1967 also cut in half a program that would have given Cleveland schools $200 per AFDC child for compensatory education. Even the U.S. Congress has failed to heed the financial plight of big city schools and for several years has not appreciably increased its grants under Title I of the Elementary and Secondary Education Act.

But financial problems are only part of the picture. Other obstacles arise from teacher inadequacies and from administration of the system itself. There is a timidity that allows the school system to rely upon conventional methods of instruction, despite their acknowledged failure, rather than seeking more innovative means. Further, the feeling among many teachers and administrators that the children of the poor are incapable of tackling more challenging work often produces student apathy and a poor self-image. There is a general lack of adequate information and experimentation about teaching the urban poor children, and especially the Negro poor children.

The schools should involve the community more in the educational process for more effective communications and understanding.

Both financial and nonfinancial problems faced by the school are largely the result of population changes that have accounted for an exodus of 127,000 residents (largely white middle class) from Cleveland between 1960 and 1965, and the immigration of 29,000 poor Negroes and Caucasians from the South where they had suffered from inadequate education.

This kind of change of student population tests the educational ability of most large Northern city school systems and presents a new set of circumstances which by its very nature demands a more innovative response.

Some insight into the shifts being demanded can be seen from sociologist Lee Rainwater's interpretation of the situation among the poor. He says the lives of the poor are dominated by two ever-present realities: deprivation and exclusion. In turn, a climate of "institutionalized pathology" is created in which the poor, separated from the rest of society, come to share the view that they are inherently worthless.[1]

This destructive pattern is evident in the classroom where teachers of the urban poor convey a feeling that these children are inadequate. Thus, when ghetto students refer to their schools as "dumbbell schools," they are echoing the false low-expectation attitude communicated to them by the teacher.

---

[1] Lee Rainwater, "Neighborhood Action and Lower Class Life Styles," in *Neighborhood Organization for Community Action,* ed. by John B. Turner, National Association of Social Workers, New York, 1968, pp. 26–27.

Children of welfare clients are further stereotyped and encounter special difficulties due to their indigency. The special costs for supplies, equipment, and activity fees, ranging from $1.85 to $18 per child or family, often cannot be met. Inadequate clothing results in high absenteeism, indeed, in dropouts. No established school policy meets these problems.

Even when help is available, as in the free school lunch program for children of clients, some children refuse the help because it identifies them as recipients. A school breakfast program helps children in 29 elementary schools, but 32 additional Title I schools are eligible but not serviced because of federal, state, and local fund shortages.

What may seem to be minor problems, it has been reported to the Commission, often create unnecessary tensions for families and the schools. For example, grades may be withheld when a child misplaces or damages a textbook and cannot make restitution because the family lacks money. A lost lunch card may mean three days without lunch because of the process of getting a replacement card from the County Welfare Department.

A speed-up of more innovative approaches started by the Cleveland schools is evidenced in the manpower approach utilized in the Woodlawn Job Center, located in the General Electric Building, for training youth for jobs. Job-related training through vocational education, though expanded by about 250% to 5,300 students in the last three years, should be accelerated with more substantial financial support.

Special attention has to be paid the ghetto school to erase its severe educational deprivation. Too many youth drop out of the ghetto schools, and those who remain end up, on an average, three to four years behind grade level in reading and other skills and "shared experiences," that is, experiences shared with pupils in some suburban schools (as described below).

Major innovations of a general nature have been suggested to cope with special ghetto school problems: compensatory enrichment programs, desegregation, and decentralization. Cleveland is substantially committed to only the first, primarily through the use of special federal grants. By and large, the results of such programs in ghetto schools in various cities have been unsatisfactory, partly because in the existing milieu teachers and pupils react with essentially the same damaging attitudes as before. Such efforts, however, cannot be dismissed.

Desegregation seeks to eliminate ghetto attitudes by eliminating the ghetto school. Various methods—changed school boundaries, educational parks, and bussing—are being tested in various cities. Integration of schools across class lines and, to a lesser extent across racial lines, is significantly associated with improved educational performance.

In Cleveland, the Supplemental Education Center has brought together upper elementary school children from different racial and class backgrounds for periodic contact, and the city has entered into limited cooperative programs of "shared experiences" with some suburban districts. Benefits of such contact are shared by children from the suburbs and the children of ghetto schools. Further, the proposed downtown high school, the new Jane Addams School, and other quality facilities can act as "magnet" schools to draw children from differing backgrounds to such facilities.

Decentralization of the school system, with concomitant sharing of control of local school operations by local area residents is too new a concept to have been tested sufficiently in practice. In this case, one seeks to capitalize on the strengths in the ghetto community by allowing the residents to have a significant voice in the education of their children. School personnel come to view ghetto students and families differently and, according to the theory, residents gain a new sense of dignity and self-worth.

It is beyond the competence of this Commission to evaluate the relative merits of these proposed solutions. Instead, the Mayor's Commission calls upon the Cleveland Board of Education to give careful consideration to all the proposals for upgrading the system within a specific time period. Necessary staff resources and funds should be allocated to this end, and recognized national experts in the field of education should be drawn upon.

FUNDING

Recommendations

- The Ohio Legislature in 1969 should amend the school foundation formula to give appropriate recognition to the heavy level of municipal and county taxation in the largest central cities of Ohio.
- The Legislature in 1969 should restore the $200 grant per AFDC child for compensatory education programs.

- The United States Congress, for the 1969 fiscal year, should materially increase its appropriation under Title I of the Elementary and Secondary Education Act.

EXPERIMENTATION

Recommendations

- The Cleveland school system should experiment with new methods of instructing disadvantaged children and accelerate the use of "integrated" teaching materials as a part of standard resources in the classroom.
- The adult education program should be preserved and expanded and its program decentralized in low-income neighborhoods.
- The Cleveland Board of Education should order whatever studies are necessary to determine the relative merits of various plans (e.g., compensatory enrichment programs, desegregation, and decentralization) for breaking the vicious circle of low expectations and self-deprecation which now permeate both *staff* and *pupil* attitudes in many ghetto schools. The Board should commit itself to act on these problems in the light of such findings and recommendations within a reasonable time period.
- Experimentation should be on a large scale and appropriate groups from the inner city should be involved in the experimentation and evaluation. Specific plans for involvement of neighborhood groups for local schools should be developed in an effort to involve parents in planning (beyond the PTA level).

TRAINING OF TEACHERS

Recommendation

- Special training programs should be provided for teachers working in low-income areas. The certification process of teachers should include provision for examination of attitudes and ability to teach children in black communities and underprivileged areas.

COMMUNITY ROLE OF SCHOOL PERSONNEL

Recommendation

- The school administration should make a major effort to

orient teachers to the special problems and needs of economically deprived children. Teachers and school administrators should be encouraged to participate in school-area community activity.

SCHOOL SYSTEM ADVOCACY, PROGRAM COORDINATION, AND COMMUNITY RELATIONS

Recommendations

- The needs of deprived children within the school system present special problems which should be dealt with in a planned and systematic manner. Personnel should be designated within the system with the specific function of giving special attention to the needs and problems of deprived children. Principals and teachers should be able to refer situations needing attention to such personnel for immediate action.
- The Cleveland school system should assign personnel to the task of coordinating and evaluating all programs related to services for welfare recipients and students from low-income families.
- The development of effective communication with the community is essential. Meetings should be held in communities with parents and interested groups on a regular basis to discuss problems and programs. This effort should be related to involving parents in the discussion of problems and in the development of meaningful action directed toward solving them.

EQUITABLE TREATMENT OF RECIPIENTS

Recommendation

- The Mayor, the School Superintendent, the County Commissioners, and the Director of the County Welfare Department should make a special effort to secure the funds necessary to provide breakfast meals for all indigent elementary school children. It is further recommended that they work out a plan for meeting clothing needs of school children on public assistance whose parents (or parent) cannot provide for them.

SCHOOL LUNCH PROGRAM

Recommendation

- County Welfare Department authorities and administrators

of the Cleveland public schools should evaluate the current practice of providing lunch cards for welfare recipients. They should be jointly responsible for developing a system which does not identify recipients of public assistance. This system should also provide for handling emergencies when lunch cards are lost in order to assure daily lunches for all needy children.

EXPANDED USE OF TITLE I FUNDS

Recommendation

- It is recommended that the Cleveland Board of Education act on behalf of indigent children by requesting a change in state regulations which restrict the use of Title I funds for special fees and purchases related to school activities. These funds should be made available for providing school supplies, special equipment and materials, and fees for educational activities.

SCHOOL LIBRARY FEES

Recommendation

- Junior and senior high school pupils from low-income families should not be punished in the event school library books are lost or damaged. Provision should be made by the school system to meet the cost of fines where students or parents cannot afford payment.

5. HEALTH

THE HEALTH PROBLEMS OF WELFARE CLIENTS

In what many consider one of the finest centers of medical care in the nation, the poor of Cleveland depend on an outmoded public health service. A good indication of the deficiency of public health in Cleveland can be seen in the state's fiscal participation in programming. The state's contribution is based on a 49-year-old law which limits its financial participation to $1,600 per health district.[1] This minimum investment in the health of the state's citizens deprives Ohio of large sums of matching federal government funds.

Without better state support the City of Cleveland will continue to find it impossible to provide adequate public health facilities. In 1963, the city expended $2,251,000 for public health services—the lowest expenditure of any major Northern city.

The lack of funds is a major reason for the paucity of services of the Cleveland Division of Health. For example, the Division has no chronic disease control or mental health program.[2] Further, the city has no epidemiological investigation or communicable disease surveillance and control unit to develop a systematic program for evaluating community health needs and the manner in which the city's health services are meeting these needs.[3]

These deficiencies become severe handicaps to the poor. Indeed, some lead indirectly not only to severe medical problems but to death. In 1966 the U.S. Commission on Civil Rights reported:

---

[1] Hughes-Griswold Act of 1919.
[2] *Local Health Organization and Staffing within Standard Metropolitan Area,* U.S. Department of Health, Education, and Welfare, 1963.
[3] *Triennial Report of Cleveland Health Department,* 1959-61.

The Crisis in Welfare in Cleveland

> Infant mortality and premature births continue to be a major problem among the non-white population of the city of Cleveland. (Although the Commission uses the non-white population, the same geographic areas have the largest concentration of welfare recipients.) The 1960–62 combined fetal and infant death rate for whites in Cleveland was 39.1 deaths per 1,000 live births. The non-white rate was 50 per cent higher at 58.3. In 1963 five Cleveland social planning areas, Central, Central-East, Central-West, Glenville, and Hough, accounted for 28.9 per cent of the city's births. Yet 60 per cent of the city's maternal deaths, 44.4 per cent of the infant deaths, 38.2 per cent of the premature births, and 48.0 per cent of the still births occurred there.[4]

The Commission also reported elsewhere:

> In 1963, 72 per cent of the mothers delivered at Metropolitan (General Hospital on the West Side) lived east of East 55th Street, a minimum distance of three and one-half miles by public transportation. A study conducted during the month of June, 1964, showed that 18.9 per cent of mothers reporting to Metropolitan to deliver babies had no prior prenatal care. Of those receiving prenatal care, the average number of visits was 4.4. While other hospitals also provide clinical services, they make it a practice not to accept any obstetrical patients beyond the third or fourth month of pregnancy.[5]

Since 1963, some hospitals, such as Mt. Sinai, have been accepting patients at any time during their pregnancy.

Although passage of Title XIX of the Social Security Act of 1965 and subsequent participation by the State of Ohio in the program makes it possible for welfare recipients to obtain the services of private physicians, few are able to avail themselves of such service. A number of reasons are apparent. Physicians now overburdened with private patients of their own are not eager to serve additional patients, especially the poor who have both a higher number of, and more severe, health problems.

The medical professionals are also unhappy—although an agreement was reached between the state and medical repre-

---

[4] Interview of Dr. Joanne E. Finley, February 26, 1966, with staff members of the U.S. Commission on Civil Rights.

[5] Hearing before the U.S. Commission on Civil Rights, April 1–7, 1966, Washington, D.C., p. 731.

sentatives—with the fee schedule which allows the state to pay only 60% of the regular fee over a minimum of $5 a visit. Some physicians, sad to say, also reflect the general public's prejudices against welfare patients and some fear that by serving the poor they may be alienating some of their regular patients. Welfare clients complain that some physicians and dentists refuse them service or make remarks they feel are humiliating.

One mother told the Commission of an experience she had had when her son was ill and she took him to a nearby hospital. She asked that her son be given a chest X ray. To her request, a physician responded, "All you welfare people want everything because you don't pay." This might have turned most welfare mothers away. But this mother insisted that her son be X-rayed. The doctor relented, and the X ray showed the boy had pneumonia. The doctor apologized for his remarks, but the attitude underlying his remark is too frequently held, even among professionals, and can affect the very care some doctors take in examining and treating a patient "on welfare."

ESTABLISHMENT OF A NEWLY STRUCTURED AND FINANCED JOINT CITY-COUNTY HEALTH DEPARTMENT

For the past 15 years the City of Cleveland increasingly has fallen behind other large urban communities in provision of all types of health services despite a large increase in population with incomes below the poverty level. Both quantitative and qualitative health care have suffered. Financial resources, especially since the state contributes so little to health care, require a broader tax base than the city presently has.

Recommendations

• At the earliest possible opportunity, the Mayor of Cleveland and the Commissioners of Cuyahoga County should prepare for the establishment of a joint City-County Health Department.
• At the earliest opportunity, a permanent Director of this Department should be appointed. (The Commission is aware of the diligent search being made for a City Director of Health.)[6]

---

[6] A City Director of Health was appointed in October, 1968.

- Because many of the health recommendations that follow will depend upon the effectiveness of this joint Department, the need for urgency in establishing the necessary budget and bringing it to the City Council and to the County Commissioners is stressed.

ESTABLISHMENT OF A COMPREHENSIVE NEIGHBORHOOD HEALTH CENTER PROGRAM

Welfare clients, as do many others, become ill, have accidents, poison themselves, conceive, have offspring, and may ultimately die in their neighborhood. Yet the services needed often are located a considerable distance from that neighborhood. This problem can be attacked by the establishment of health facilities within or near the neighborhood and by adequate transportation, where necessary.

Recommendations

- The Mayor's Commission recommends that the County Health Department move more quickly to establish a series of multipurpose neighborhood health centers in the city. The centers shall include a variety of social, as well as health services. The communities requiring immediate action are: the West Side, the Hough neighborhood (a Hough-86th Street Health Center is in the planning stages), and the Central, Glenville, and Mt. Pleasant areas.
- The four major hospital centers providing health services to the poor (University, Metropolitan General, Mt. Sinai, St. Luke's) should seek the participation either of those larger hospitals currently not now providing health services to the poor or of smaller neighborhood hospitals that do not have adequate resources to provide the necessary support to comprehensive multipurpose neighborhood health centers.

DATA PROCESSING CENTERS FOR HEALTH RECORDS OF THE MEDICALLY INDIGENT

A prime defect in servicing welfare clients in the health field is the lack of continuity of individual health information. This results from the piecemeal and fragmented health services available to clients. Often one medical service outlet has no knowledge of the client's prior medical history. This lack of communication is wasteful, makes duplication of work necessary, and, more important, may be critical in providing quality care.

Recommendations

- The present Academy of Medicine Committee be activated as the *pro forma* agency to coordinate data processing from the Cleveland Health Department, the Board of Education, the County hospital system, and the large voluntary hospital systems.
- Moreover, it is recommended that, at the earliest opportunity, legal opinion be obtained to determine who has what rights in connection with privileged communication of health information and of the rights of privacy of the medically indigent.

ESTABLISHMENT OF A JOINT WELFARE-HEALTH SERVICES TRAINING PROGRAM

The increased use of allied workers and subprofessionals in the health delivery system and the movement toward comprehensive health centers requires that a wider range of persons be acquainted with the health service available and how it can be obtained. This is particularly true of social workers who will be referring clients for medical services.

Recommendations

- In conjunction with the formation of a joint City-County Health Department, a joint welfare health service training facility should be established to increase the effectiveness of services to the medically indigent.
- In the event recommended changes in Title XIX legislation are not immediately forthcoming, the city administration should consult with large third-party health insurers to establish voluntary prepaid health services for welfare clients and the medically indigent.

IMPROVEMENT OF HEALTH SERVICES IN THE SCHOOLS

As with other health services, many welfare clients feel health services in the schools are deficient. They note the inability of the school health program to provide simple treatment of minor accidents and injuries and minimum treatment of common but simple illnesses, such as pyoderma, where a skin culture and throat culture might easily be provided by a school nurse.

Thus, it is the recommendation of the Mayor's Commission that the Director of Health Services of the Cleveland Board of Education should act to improve the quality of health services of school nurses in three specific areas that are deficient.

Recommendations

• School nurses should be encouraged to play an important, professional, correlative role between teachers and the Board of Education diagnostic services, such as psychological, speech and hearing, and dental services. The absence of any such correlative agency or person at this time tends to decrease considerably the effectiveness of such services for many families in the inner city.

• Also, school nurses should assume a more active role in referral, follow-up, and continuity of those school children who become either acutely ill or have accidents. It should be the legal responsibility of school nurses to see that such children's parents are notified and that, if an emergency situation exists, the child is taken, under school health supervision, to an adequate facility for diagnosis and treatment.

• Further, the school nurses should assume responsibility for simple diagnostic tests, such as throat cultures and skin cultures, available at no cost through other health services in the community. This would considerably increase the effectiveness of preventive diagnostic services and considerably enhance the effectiveness of the Rheumatic Fever Prevention Program of the Heart Association of Northeastern Ohio.

DEFINITION OF RESPONSIBILITY OF THE NEWLY ESTABLISHED COMPREHENSIVE HEALTH PLANNING AGENCY TO HEALTH CARE OF THE MEDICALLY INDIGENT

The Mayor's Commission expects the newly established comprehensive health planning agency to be a proper vehicle for the advance of medical care of the entire community. It also expects that particular efforts will be made in establishing and meeting the needs of welfare clients and the medically indigent.

Thus the Commission stresses the need for the comprehensive health planning agency to include suitable programs for the medically indigent in its program. Particularly urgent are the following: revision of adequate dental health care resources, both of a prophylactic screening nature and a restorative nature; provision of adequate evaluation and treatment of mental illness in the medically poor; and the establishment of other federal programs specifically directed toward certain population groups.

For example, the U.S. Children's Bureau has funded children and youth programs to be developed and administered by a University medical center to provide comprehensive health services to infants and children throughout adolescence. In Philadelphia five such programs are presently being administered by the five medical schools there, providing an extensive enrichment of medical care to this target population. Similar programs are available which require prompt investigation.

INCREASE IN FUNDS AND POPULATION COVERAGE OF THE TITLE XIX PROGRAM

One intent of legislation establishing Title XIX medical assistance was to provide a choice of medical services for the indigent population. The present fee situation discourages participation of doctors and dentists and defeats a major purpose of the Medicaid program. There is a need for health screening and preventive medical service to reduce the incidence of health problems among the poor.

Recommendations

- The Commission recommends that the Governor and State Legislature take immediate steps to broaden the coverage of the Title XIX program so as to include *all* medically indigent individuals and families.
- In addition, the fee schedule should be revised to provide a level of remuneration to medical and dental professionals, which would be an incentive to treating welfare recipients and other poor.
- Provision must be made for screening and preventive services in an effort to reduce the incidence of serious health problems and over-all cost of medical services to the poor.

6. HOUSING

In 1967, a Cleveland citizens group investigated the housing problem in the metropolitan area and concluded that a "crisis" in housing exists. According to the group's report,[1] some 60,000 units of housing, most of them located in the city, are substandard. For racial and economic reasons, low-income families, with a high proportion on public assistance, live in the neighborhoods where the high concentration of substandard housing exists.

In addition to the hardships associated with poor physical structures, low-income families are subject to other deficiencies, all too evident in these neighborhoods. These include poor health and education facilities, inadequate schools, high concentration of crime, inadequate city services, lack of recreation and other modern amenities, and an across-the-board overtaxing of community facilities because of high population concentration.

The physical structures themselves contribute to economic and psychological problems. For instance, although public assistance recipients receive a small, set allowance for utility expenses, the poor housing conditions ensure that these services will cost them more than in a newer housing unit. An average family of four receives a total of $20 for utilities, yet the heating alone often costs as much as $60 a month during the winter, due to poor condition of window sashes, improper or nonexisting insulation, and deficient heating facilities. The attempt by the client to continue payment and avoid cutoff of service keeps the family under constant economic pressure throughout the year.

Public housing was created to house low-income families in

---

[1] *Report of the Plan of Action for Tomorrow's Housing* (PATH), Cleveland, 1967.

decent, safe, and sanitary conditions. However, public housing has failed to serve many public assistance families for several reasons. First, the city and the community combined to prevent the spread of such housing throughout the city. Second, cost of construction and limitations on federal funds hindered activity. Third, there was a crisis in housing for the elderly, which the city housing authority tried to fill and which the community was willing to accept. However, there was not community acceptance of expansion of public housing for the families with children that urgently needed such housing. Public housing has been limited also by the City Council, which has refused to allow public housing in many areas of the city where land might be more readily available and at lesser cost to the taxpayer, and by the suburbs. Less than 7% (2,127)[2] of the 31,000 families receiving public assistance in the county are housed in public housing projects.

Although a number of new federal programs have been instituted since the public housing law, none has been able to produce more than a trickle of housing at a cost low enough for low-income families. Although many states have legislation that helps relieve the problems of low- and middle-income families in housing, Ohio has been totally lacking in legislation or financial assistance to cities in this area.

Cleveland itself has contributed to the problem by lack of enforcement of its housing code. And, though a housing court exists in Cleveland Municipal Court, improvement in its operation is necessary, including the assignment of jurisdiction over all cases involving legal questions related to housing.

INCREASING PUBLIC HOUSING UNITS

Recommendations

• The Cleveland Metropolitan Housing Authority should make immediate plans to construct 5,000 additional housing units with substantial numbers of three-, four-, and five-bedroom apartments to supplement the presently planned 2,500.

---

[2]Report from Director of County Welfare Housing Department. The report shows the following number of families in public housing by financial assistance category: Aid for the Aged, 580; Aid for the Disabled, 30; Aid to Families with Dependent Children, 1,111; Aid to Dependent Children of the Unemployed, 144; Soldiers and Sailors Relief, 31; and General Relief, 231.

- Priority should be given to leasing private housing city-wide.
- Service centers should be within public housing estates to accommodate public and private agencies in a range of services, including family counseling, day care, homemaking, and budgeting.

SUBURBAN HOUSING OPPORTUNITIES

The Mayor's Commission recommends that the following steps be taken to allow public housing and rent supplement programs in suburban areas to open better housing to welfare clients and low-income families.

Recommendations
- Each suburban government should pass ordinances to permit construction and leasing of public housing through the Cleveland Metropolitan Housing Authority.
- Each suburb should develop a workable program and thereby expand the use of rent supplements in developing housing for low-income families.
- Each suburb should pass strong open housing ordinances and institute the means of implementation.

CLEVELAND CITY COUNCIL

The Commission recommends enactment of an ordinance to allow leasing of housing by the Cleveland Metropolitan Housing Authority on a city-wide basis.

HOUSING CODE ENFORCEMENT

Recommendations
- The city should immediately begin strict enforcement of the housing code. The effort should be bolstered by additional inspectors and better training. Prompt action should be taken to prosecute habitual violators. In addition, the Cleveland Law Department should use the mandatory injunction procedure under Section 715.30 of the Ohio Revised Code.
- The Housing Court should be reorganized and strengthened, to the extent possible under present law, by increasing its authority to cover all legal matters related to offenders. In addi-

tion, the city should ask the Ohio Legislature to enact sufficient state-enabling legislation to strengthen the court.

STATE LEGISLATION

The Commission recommends that the Mayor of Cleveland request state-enabling legislation and constitutional changes, where relevant, to provide local options for dealing with housing problems as follows:

Recommendations

- Legislation should be enacted to permit the city to acquire and rehabilitate substandard properties when landlords are chronic violators of the code or unable to make needed repairs. Such properties should be managed by a receiver and scrutinized by the courts until such time as the receiver has been reimbursed through rents collected. Following reimbursement, these properties would be returned to the owners.
- The Ohio Constitution should be amended to permit the city to provide tax rebates for new construction or major rehabilitation of substandard properties for people of low income. Enabling legislation pursuant to such an amendment should provide for reimbursement to the city for tax abatement. This would encourage new construction and private rehabilitation of properties in deteriorating areas.
- The County Welfare Department should be empowered to withhold rents from landlords when serious housing violations are permitted to exist in buildings where public assistance recipients reside.

ADVOCACY FOR TENANTS

Recommendation

- The Cuyahoga County Welfare Department and the Cleveland Department of Community Development should encourage and support tenants in withholding rents when landlords refuse to correct flagrant code violations. This action should be taken in situations where owners have been given ample time to correct violations cited by housing inspectors. The County Welfare Department would be acting in the public interest by supporting an action which prevents the use of public money to subsidize misery, blight, and urban decay.

7. PUBLIC-VOLUNTARY RELATIONSHIPS

The Mayor's Commission examined the relationship of the private to the public sector in welfare. One line of inquiry was aimed at getting a perspective on the total welfare investments and their distribution from both sectors. Up-to-date statistics are not available. The last complete set of data, for 1965, show that for welfare services alone, 79% of the total funds expended in Cuyahoga County came from public sources, and 21% from private sources. Only about one-third of the sums from private sources (7.6% of the total) derives from the combined contributions from the United Appeal and sectarian funds, the remainder from fees, endowments, and other income.[1]

The major investment of private funds is in the health area, where 69.7% of all income is from fees for service. On the public side, welfare services account for 55.7% of all expenditures in the County.[2] If all programs, including social insurance, veterans programs, and welfare, health, and recreation services are taken into account, public funds account for 70.6% of expenditures; United Appeal and other contributions account for 3.2%; the remaining 26.2% are from fees and other income.

In Cleveland's poverty areas live 19% of Cuyahoga County's population; 25% of the funds of voluntary agencies (from all sources, including but not restricted to United Appeal funds) and 74% of public funds for welfare[3] are distributed in these same areas.

Distribution of expenditures by the private agencies tends to follow the population distribution; there is, however, added emphasis in the poverty areas particularly by "local group

---

[1] Table Q.1a (Appendix Q).
[2] Table Q.2.
[3] Table Q.4.

service" agencies, such as the Greater Cleveland Neighborhood Centers Association, Karamu House, the Phillis Wheatley Association, and Garden Valley Neighborhood House. It was not possible to determine exactly how the proportion of aid from the United Appeal itself is distributed among the agencies in relation to the income level of recipients of service affected by such aid, since statistics have been kept on the basis of the section of the city (census tract) where the client resides, rather than on the basis of his economic level. It is evident that many poor people reside in areas not designated as poverty areas, and many residents of poverty areas are not poor; there are voluntary agencies outside of designated poverty areas which serve poor people, and there are agencies within poverty areas which include other than poor among the people served.

Increasing priority has been given over the past few years— to the extent that options were available for fund distribution —to agencies serving poverty area clientele. This has been particularly true of the support given the local group service agencies, over 50% of whose clientele is concentrated in the depressed areas of the city. The United Appeal is a prime source of their support.

The national group service agencies, such as the Boy Scouts, YMCA, and YWCA, by contrast, expend 11% of their funds in poverty areas, and only 12% of their clientele are from such parts of the city.

A relatively small part of the total population is reached by the private sector in welfare service as a whole. This is true even in such functions as counseling, where the private sector carries almost the entire burden. Lack of funds and personnel largely explain these shortcomings. For economic assistance the public sector carries the entire responsibility.

The Commission recognizes the significant contributions made to Greater Cleveland social welfare programs under both voluntary and public auspices. It believes that the private sector should be much more amply supported.

The Commission considers the present relationship between public and private services as not yet constituting a genuine partnership for an attack on the welfare problems of Greater Cleveland. The voluntary sector has important functions, but neither its resources nor its services can be equated with the public services that are required to meet the needs of the poor in Cleveland.

The huge need for economic and related assistance can neither be met nor prevented by the private sector. Public agencies have the responsibility but have not been able to meet it. The voluntary agencies have neither been able to fill the gap nor, despite the efforts that have been made, have they been successful in mobilizing effective support for the public sector.

The function of the private sector should be understood as more than contributing certain important services. It should be regarded as part of a public-voluntary social welfare system, in touch with a large and prestigious constituency, which could become the means of advancing the community's general welfare. The private sector has a vital, fundamental, and vigilant role to play. It must be organized so as to ensure that the community as a whole provides the taxing authorities with the means and the will to meet their obligations to those in need. This role, in our judgment, has not yet been adequately fulfilled. Although certain dedicated laymen have assumed broad and earnestly committed responsibilities in welfare, the leadership of voluntary agencies as a whole has tended to speak primarily for the interests of their agencies but has not effectively involved their constituencies in major efforts to improve the total standards of welfare in the community. Legislators and administrative bodies will take necessary action only when they sense strong public support and not on the basis of occasional resolutions from committees or boards of trustees.

The voluntary agencies have important roles not only in innovation, demonstration, and research but, particularly, in advocacy in relation to clients in poverty areas. They are also in a position to test new services which can be adopted by the public sector if they are proved successful.

Many more efforts than have yet been developed should be undertaken to make available to public agencies the knowledge and skill disproportionately represented within the private sector. Although the overwhelming amount of expenditures for welfare services are under public agency auspices, the overwhelming proportion of professional social work manpower (i.e., those with graduate social work education) is employed in the private agencies. The latter have, on the whole, been organized to give high-quality services, utilizing professionally trained manpower with graduate social work education. These services, however, particularly in counseling, are either inaccessible or for other reasons relatively unused by the poverty population. The inequity of the distribution of highly skilled manpower between the public and private agencies requires special attention. The primary responsibility to meet the basic needs of people rests with the public sector, but the discrepancies in access to manpower are such as to make the fulfillment of this responsibility most difficult.

There should be research knowledge accumulated by the private agencies which would be of value to the planning of public services. Private agencies are in a position to play an advocacy role for poverty clients in relation both to private and public services. Private welfare cannot, through its direct services, be expected to meet the basic needs of people for food, clothing, and shelter. It can, however, provide the initial impetus for developing new programs and community support, for conducting research, for experimenting with innovations in delivery of service, and for sharing manpower to assist the public agencies in providing the means to meet the overwhelming and pressing needs of people on public welfare.

Recommendations

• The leadership of the private sector, including all private agencies and not only those within the Welfare Federation of Cleveland, should assume increasing responsibility for assuring adequate financial resources to meet basic human welfare needs. As one way of furthering this goal, each voluntary agency should form a Public Welfare or Public Affairs Committee to help mobilize sufficient financial and legislative support so that these human needs can be met. These committees should work in close cooperation with one another and be coordinated with the Public Welfare Committee of the Welfare Federation. The latter Committee should include representatives of welfare clientele and should serve as spokesman on public welfare for the entire constituency of voluntary agencies.

• The Welfare Federation of Cleveland should be the spearhead for testing in the courts current restrictions on state welfare standards and performance in order to raise standards to an adequate level and enhance the entire area of public welfare service.

• Budget allocations by the Welfare Federation should reflect even more the commitment of the private agencies to the function of involving their constituency in the problems of public

welfare, in innovation and demonstration, in service, in research, and in advocacy in relation to the poor.
• Both voluntary and public agencies require more attention to evaluation of their services. Public agencies on county and state levels should develop greater research resources and competence for data gathering, analysis, and evaluation, with an eye to continuous assessment of effectiveness and identifying unmet needs.
• Interagency programs should be expanded between public and private agencies that would provide the public agencies with access to the more highly skilled personnel presently concentrated in the private agencies.
• The proposed Urban Coalition should assign a high priority for action to the issue of welfare.

8. COUNCIL FOR ECONOMIC OPPORTUNITY

The Economic Opportunity Act of 1964 was hailed as a major American attack on poverty. Three and one-half years later that hope has nearly vanished. Severe cuts by Congress and attacks by the public have gravely reduced whatever effectiveness the "war on poverty" might have had.

The Commission on the Crisis in Welfare has not attempted to evaluate the entire program of the Council for Economic Opportunity (CEO) but has been particularly concerned with those areas of activity such as Outreach work, which permit new insights into the problems of poverty and particularly with the problems of those on welfare.

A principal function for a poverty program is advocacy of the poor. Although this function should be built into all efforts of the Council, the Commission finds it lacking. Despite the revelations by Outreach workers of major problems with institutions and government agencies faced by the poor, almost nothing of this has been brought to the attention of the public, and no major changes have been accomplished.

The CEO Board of Directors, made up of a cross section of the community, has not responded, nor has it been in a position to respond, to these deficiencies. It should be revitalized and its role should be reinterpreted. Sufficiently ample funds for relevant research and evaluation also have been lacking, although there have been serious efforts to build up these functions.

Recommendations

• It is recommended that the Council for Economic Opportunity create within its structure a program designed to have an advocacy role for the poor. This advocacy should include: the hearing and evaluating of complaints from the community regarding conditions of the poor; evaluating failures of service systems to provide needed services supporting the advocacy role of Outreach workers; and working to effect changes in service systems where needed.

a) Personnel involved in the above tasks should periodically make reports to the CEO Board and issue releases to the public media regarding CEO activities and findings. As a result of the information provided through this program, the Board should attempt to use community resources to effect changes in institutions and agencies that fail in their service responsibilities to the public. The experiences of the poor, as revealed through the community feedback system, should be a major source of information for planning and developing new services in both the public and private sectors.

b) Personnel should be assigned to monitor continuously and evaluate the various programs which are supported by CEO funds.

• The Director of CEO should seek additional research funds from public and private sources to provide for adequate evaluation of CEO and delegate agency services in poverty areas. The entire evaluative process of delegate agencies should be under the auspices and direction of the CEO Research Department.

• Planning and evaluation of current and proposed programs should involve utilization of the poor who are recipients of services. Their involvement should be on a meaningful level of participating in all levels of decision-making, and they should be representative of community groups concerned with problems of the poor.

PART III
CONCLUSIONS

9. SUMMARY OF MAJOR RECOMMENDATIONS BY LEVEL

FEDERAL

- Legislate a national program of income guarantees and supplements, assuring a budgetary standard at least at the federally determined "poverty line level" for all needy families and individuals—and as soon as possible at a higher level of adequacy—with a policy of guaranteed employment for all who can work, the federal government being the employer of last resort. (Congress)
- Remove mandatory employment provision for AFDC mothers in present Social Security law. (Congress)
- Repeal freeze on AFDC children caseloads. (Congress)
- Establish regulations to protect rights of working mothers. (Departments of Labor and Health, Education, and Welfare)
- Provide inspection and evaluation of training programs, work sites, and day care centers to ensure high standards. (Departments of Labor and Health, Education, and Welfare)
- Make AFDC for employed fathers mandatory in all states. (Congress)

STATE

- Set new budget standards for welfare above the poverty line. Such a minimum standard should also be set nationally. (State Department of Public Welfare)
- Provide substantial increase in state revenue through equitable state income tax on personal and corporate income. (General Assembly, Governor)
- Achieve maximum participation in Title XIX of Medicare. (General Assembly, Governor)

- Increase staff and budget of Ohio Civil Rights Commission. (General Assembly, Governor)
- Strengthen Ohio Civil Rights Commission's investigatory powers relating to discrimination in employment, training, and housing. (General Assembly, Governor)
- Initiate legislation to permit cities to acquire and rehabilitate substandard properties when landlord chronically violates code. (General Assembly, Governor)
- Amend the Ohio Constitution so as to permit cities to provide tax rebates for major rehabilitation of substandard properties. (General Assembly, Governor)
- Establish regulations to protect rights of welfare mothers affected by new Social Security legislation. (Department of Employment Security)
- Expedite speedy and efficient delivery of checks to clients by use of advanced management techniques. (Department of Public Welfare)
- Simplify eligibility process by use of simple declaration of income. (Department of Public Welfare)
- Develop simplified *client* handbook of rights and responsibilities. (State Department of Public Welfare)
- Provide simplified *manual* of rights and responsibilities of clients and agencies. (Department of Public Welfare)
- Create State Welfare Board with client representation. (Department of Public Welfare)
- Reorganize and strengthen Housing Court. (General Assembly)

COUNTY

- Withhold client rents when serious housing violations are not corrected. (County Welfare Department)
- Activate and expand County Welfare Advisory Board with significant client representation. (County Commissioners and Director of County Welfare Department)
- Modify fair hearing process to protect client's rights and extend fair hearing to General Relief. (County Welfare Department)
- Separate income maintenance from delivery of social services. (County Welfare Department)
- Decentralize services at neighborhood level. (County Welfare Department)

- Study feasibility of Joint City-County Health Department. (County Commissioners)
- Establish multipurpose health and social service centers in neighborhoods throughout the city. (County Commissioners, Metropolitan General Hospital)
- Innovate joint health and welfare training programs for medical and social service personnel working with medically indigent patients. (County Commissioners, hospitals)
- Creation of day care facilities at places of employment for all who need them. (County Commissioners)
- Greater evaluation for proper accountability relating to effectiveness, efficiency, and relevance of programs toward betterment of community. (County Welfare Department)
- Expansion of interagency programs between public and private agencies to provide public agencies with highly skilled personnel. (County Welfare Department, Welfare Federation of Cleveland)

CITY

- Appoint official to represent the interests of the city's welfare clientele. (Mayor)
- Study feasibility of Joint City-County Health Department. (Mayor, County Commissioners)
- Establish multipurpose health and social service centers in neighborhoods throughout the city. (Mayor, County Commissioners, Council for Economic Opportunity, Welfare Federation of Cleveland, University Hospital, Metropolitan General Hospital, Mt. Sinai Hospital, St. Luke's Hospital)
- Innovate joint health and welfare training programs for medical and social service personnel working with medically indigent patients. (Hospitals, professional schools of medicine and social work, Mayor, County Commissioners)
- Improve quality of health services to school children by expanding duties and responsibilities of school nurses. (Board of Education)
- Substantially increase the number of public housing units above the 2,500 now planned, primarily through leasing private housing on a city-wide basis. (Cleveland Metropolitan Housing Authority)
- Enact ordinances to facilitate city-wide leasing by Cleveland Metropolitan Housing Authority. (City Council)

- Expand summer youth employment to full-time employment. (Mayor, Greater Cleveland Growth Association, National Alliance of Businessmen)
- Intensify efforts to serve as advocates for poor in relation to other service systems. (Council for Economic Opportunity)
- Evaluate effectiveness of CEO programs. (Council for Economic Opportunity)
- Provide for greater utilization of poor in planning and evaluating CEO programs. (Council for Economic Opportunity)
- Revitalize CEO Board. (Mayor)
- Initiate large-scale experimentation in desegregation, decentralization, and innovative enrichment programs as means for breaking pattern of low expectations and self-depreciation of ghetto students and staff. (Cleveland Board of Education)
- Expand breakfast programs so as to include all needy children. (Board of Education)
- Administer school lunch program so as to avoid embarrassment of welfare recipients. (Board of Education)
- Establish more effective communication with parents and neighborhood groups. (Board of Education)
- Spur creation of industrial locations in ghetto areas. (Mayor, Greater Cleveland Growth Association)
- Seek federal funds for special job placement programs for people seeking service-related employment. (Mayor)
- Intensify efforts to expand job market and training programs for women. (Mayor, Greater Cleveland Growth Association, National Alliance of Businessmen)
- Create day care facilities at places of employment for all who need them. (Mayor, County Commissioners, Greater Cleveland Growth Association)
- Study feasibility of providing transportation for workers from inner city to outlying industrial parks. (Mayor, Greater Cleveland Growth Association)
- Pass ordinances to permit construction and leasing of public housing. (Suburban governments)
- Pass open occupancy ordinances with appropriate enforcement machinery. (Suburban governments)
- Provide for strict enforcement of housing code and prompt prosecution of habitual violators. (City Law Department)
- Reorganize and strengthen Housing Court. (City Council, Ohio General Assembly—for enabling legislation)

PRIVATE SECTOR

- Establish multipurpose health and social service centers in neighborhoods throughout the city. (Council for Economic Opportunity, Welfare Federation of Cleveland, Mt. Sinai Hospital, St. Luke's Hospital, University Hospital)
- Innovate joint health and welfare training programs for medical and social service personnel working with medically indigent patients. (Hospitals, professional schools of medicine and social work)
- Expand summer youth employment to full-time employment. (Greater Cleveland Growth Association, National Alliance of Businessmen)
- Spur creation of industrial locations in ghetto areas. (Greater Cleveland Growth Association)
- Intensify efforts to expand job market and training programs for women. (Greater Cleveland Growth Association, National Alliance of Businessmen)
- Create day care facilities at places of employment for all who need them. (Greater Cleveland Growth Association)
- Create Public Welfare or Public Affairs Committee to mobilize financial and legislative support for basic human welfare needs. (Greater Cleveland Growth Association, National Alliance of Businessmen)
- Test cases in courts on state welfare standards and performance. (Welfare Federation of Cleveland)
- Increase involvement of voluntary agency constituency in the problems of public welfare. (Welfare Federation of Cleveland)
- Expand interagency programs between public and private agencies to provide public agencies with highly skilled personnel. (Welfare Federation of Cleveland, County Welfare Department)
- Make welfare follow-up an agenda priority in the proposed Urban Coalition. (Private sector, City)

CONCLUDING NOTE

The welfare crisis is real. It is composed of many facets: an outmoded national welfare system, made even less workable by restrictive interpretations and low levels of financial support by the State of Ohio; grossly inadequate financial assistance for families and their children; apathy or ignorance of the facts about the poor on welfare by the public at large; prejudice against those on public assistance in general, compounded by race prejudice; failures in housing, health care, education, employment, and job training. All of these add up to misery for those compelled to receive public assistance.

The resolutions proposed are of two kinds. The first is concerned with reforms that should be put into effect immediately to make the present welfare system and other parts of our social structure more responsive to the needs of the poor and that will lead to a greater sense of dignity and self-reliance. The purpose of the second group of resolutions is to help us to move as rapidly as possible toward a basic overhauling of our national income maintenance system for the poor by providing a guaranteed annual income floor below which no American income should fall. This floor should be set at least at the federally determined poverty line level.

All parts of the community are involved in welfare, because all are affected by it. All have a contribution to make to constructive changes. If we persist in maintaining a predominantly "don't care" attitude in our society, we shall reap a harvest of anger and despair, and we shall fail to break the dreadful cycle of poverty.

Welfare and income maintenance alone will not break this cycle. It will take changes in every major sector of our society to make sure that we do not perpetuate poverty and dependency. But the rock-bottom floor for all such efforts is some decent economic basis for life.

APPENDIXES

APPENDIX A
LETTER FROM MAYOR CARL B. STOKES, APPOINTING THE COMMISSION ON THE CRISIS IN WELFARE

City of Cleveland

CARL B STOKES
MAYOR

December 28, 1967

Dear Dr. Stein:

As you know, I have been giving much thought to the steps that must be taken to bring about more adequate solutions to the crisis in public welfare appropriations in Cleveland and Ohio in general. During my legislative years, much of my time was devoted to seeking adequate standards and supporting appropriations for those standards for welfare recipients.

As Mayor of the City of Cleveland, I now hope to take steps which will be helpful in solving this critical and tragic inadequacy. It is my intention to create a Commission On the Crisis in Welfare to be composed of representatives of private and public leadership in Cleveland, the religious community which has often been active toward solving the problem, and members of the poverty community itself. I am charging this Commission to determine just what the situation of needy children is, how it got that way, and what should be done about it. Moreover, I am requesting the Commission to examine the relationship of government to this situation at municipal, county, state and Federal levels. I am asking that the relationship of voluntary philanthropy, business, labor, the professions and the public at large be studied in detail.

I have been assured of the full cooperation of the County Commissioners in this study and have been encouraged to believe that religious and other organizations might supply funds, unavailable in the city budget, to support this Commission's work.

- 2 -

Because of your distinguished national reputation in the field of health and welfare problems, I would be pleased if you would accept the chairmanship of this Commission. You may be confident of my full support of the Commission's efforts and the complete cooperation of my staff within the limits of their legitimate responsibilities within the government of the city.

Attached to this letter is my proposed list of the membership of the Commission. It is my hope that they might be quickly convened and appropriate staff employed as soon as possible. I hope the Commission might present its findings to me and to the general public by June of 1968.

I do hope you will accept this position with the Commission.

Yours sincerely,

Carl B. Stokes

Dr. Herman D. Stein, Provost
  of Social and Behavioral Sciences
Case Western Reserve University
Room 37, Adelbert Main Building
Cleveland, Ohio 44106

APPENDIX B
MYTHS AND REALITIES IN WELFARE

Public welfare and its recipients have become the victims of the general public's stereotypes, prejudices, and antagonisms—a grotesque cartoon portrayal of a welfare state squandering the taxpayer's wealth upon the undeserving.

This bias has a long history, fortified frequently by mass media and the natural human feelings of the haves towards the have-nots. There has thus developed an increasingly large gap between myth and reality. The Mayor's Commission on the Crisis in Welfare has taken a look at some of the most prevalent myths in an effort to close the credibility gap.

The result reveals that the welfare client is not the offender but the victim.

MYTH: *The solution to the welfare problem is for people to get a job.*

"I fight poverty, I've got a job," says one of the new protest buttons.

Indeed, the rising affluence of the American people can readily be seen. But studies have shown that this rising affluence through increasing productivity, employment, and income has not much effect on the fortunes of welfare recipients. In fact, the number of people receiving assistance has grown during a time of general rising affluence.

The advantage of rising employment and increased national wealth is "reaped automatically only by those who are in a position to take employment."[1]

Welfare recipients are not in a position to take employment and thus have not shared in the growing abundance of national wealth. As we have already seen, a 1968 analysis of the Cuyahoga County Welfare Department revealed that 96% of its

---

[1] Eveline M. Burns, "The Future Course of Public Welfare," paper presented at the Governor's Conference to Help Plan New Approaches to Welfare in the United States, October, 1967, p. 12.

public assistance recipients were unemployable; 65% were children under the age of 18 years; 18% were mothers or grandmothers with child care responsibilities; 10% were aged; 4.5% were permanently or totally disabled and/or blind; only 3% were unemployed fathers who might become employable.[2]

Similarly, a Presidential report on the state of employability of welfare recipients nationally, showed that a mere 1% could be employed and then only if proper training and other factors were available.

One may ask why the recipients are not able to be employed. Some reasons are obvious. Children in the American society are no longer expected to work as they once were. Thus if children—the majority of recipients—were to be put to work it would require a drastic change in laws and tradition.

But a major reason lies with our society's tragic legacy of prejudice, ignorance, and exploitation, which has left the great majority of adults on welfare poorly equipped for employment by training, education, and even general health. They are thus unemployable. In addition, though affluence is evident, the largest reduction of unemployment has been concentrated among the higher skilled job categories.[3]

MYTH: *The many women on welfare can work if they wanted to.*

Much of the public ire toward the welfare system is directed toward mothers in need. However, 90% of AFDC families have a woman as sole head of the family, according to study of such families in Cuyahoga County.[4] The study indicates that almost all of the 90% have at least one child under 6 years of age. Thus, in order for the woman to take full-time employment, if she could get it, some provision must be made for the children.

Only 10% of the working mothers used day care facilities for child care, both because of the high cost and the lack of adequate facilities, according to the study. The study also revealed that inadequate preparation for jobs kept mothers from achieving employment. Less than 10% of the mothers had any vocational training experience. While 18% of the mothers receiving assistance had completed high school, more than 26%

---

[2]Cuyahoga County Welfare Department report, January, 1968.
[3]Burns, "The Future Course of Public Welfare."
[4]*Preliminary Study of Characteristics of AFDC Population,* Cuyahoga County Welfare Department, April, 1968.

had completed less than an eighth grade education. Of the 80% who had some work experience, fewer than 10% worked in occupations that could be classified as even semiskilled.

Another problem relates to poor health. More than 40% of the welfare clients (both men and women) referred to Title V (a work training program) since 1965 were found by doctors to be unable to hold a job for health reasons. In addition, more than 50% of those accepted were found to be in need of medical attention.[5]

MYTH: *If relief payments are kept low, clients will be compelled to seek jobs or other means of support.*

If this myth had any basis in truth, there would be no welfare crisis in Ohio. The U.S. Commission on Civil Rights after a study of the Cuyahoga County Welfare AFDC program declared that the program was "grossly inadequate to provide support and care requisite for health and decency."

In fact, welfare payments are lower proportionately today than they were in 1960 in Ohio, yet the number of clients has increased steadily.

Actually, the lower relief payments have merely been more destructive, both physically and psychologically, to welfare families and have worked contrary to the spirit of Ohio law and the stated philosophy that welfare be an incentive to "self-improvement." A New York City study revealed that 65% of the mothers receiving public assistance said that they often had feelings of "despair and resignation."

By deliberately maintaining payments below what the state itself sets as a minimum subsistence level, the system encourages fraud, prostitution, and other exploitive relationships.[6] Indeed, the children subjected to this life environment tend to develop self-defeating attitudes toward education, work, and their future. This perpetuates dependency and continues the poverty cycle the welfare program supposedly aims to break.[7]

A feeling of security is most important to low-income families and serves to offset the constant state of tension and the

---

[5] Memorandum on Title V Program, Cuyahoga County Welfare Department, November, 1967.

[6] Jack Roach, "The Culture of Poverty," *Journal of Social Forces,* March, 1967.

[7] Lee Rainwater, "Crucible of Identity: The Negro Lower-Class Family," *Daedalus,* Vol. 95, No. 1 (Winter, 1966).

unpredictable pressures of daily life. Low payments, below any level of decency, promote insecurity, thus subverting individual initiative and ambition. The feeling that one has no control over his destiny becomes one of the tragic consequences of the low payments.[8]

MYTH: *Many who receive public assistance have income sources and are receiving payments by fraud.*

If it were not so sad, it would be amusing to note that every study made to determine the extent of fraud in public assistance has cost more to produce than the amount of fraud uncovered.

Indeed, comparisons of fraud among the poor with fraud by the general public in income tax reporting reveals many sectors of the general public to be more inviting of suspicion and control than the poor.

Extensive investigation of AFDC families in Ohio in 1963, conducted by the U.S. Department of Health, Education, and Welfare, indicated that of the 37,000 families then on public assistance, 5% were ineligible. Further, of the payments made in error, 42% were underpayments to clients, while 28% were overpayments. The net effect of under- and overpayments showed that the clients lost more money than they gained as a group, and the state benefited by the mistakes.

Rather than conforming to the stereotype of cheats, welfare clients may well be considered above average in honesty. For example, the County Welfare Department estimated that welfare clients in Cuyahoga County would report about $802,000 in income for 1967, a notable fact when one considers that these funds were deducted from payments already below subsistence levels.

While studies estimate suspected fraud in welfare to be between 9% and 16%, Internal Revenue frauds, as reported by economic researchers to Congress in 1959, run as high as 34% (Table B.1).

MYTH: *Welfare recipients are content with their positions. Many prefer welfare as an easy way of life without work.*

There is evidence from both Cleveland and New York that clients want to achieve personal and economic independence as soon as possible. In New York City, when a large sample of

---

[8]J. S. Coleman, *et al., Equality of Educational Opportunity,* U.S. Department of Health, Education, and Welfare, Office of Education, 1966.

Table B.1. Internal Revenue Frauds, 1959

Groups	TOTAL FUNDS DEFRAUDED (MILLIONS OF DOLLARS)	PERCENTAGE OF CATEGORY COMMITTING FRAUD
Farmers	5,000	28%
Small businessmen, plus professionals (doctors, lawyers, etc.)	7,000	28
Wage and salary earners	6,500	3
Receivers of interest	2,800	34
Receivers of dividends	900	8
Receivers of pensions and annuities	600	29
Receivers of rent, royalties, and other capital gains	1,200	11

SOURCE: Philip M. Stern, *Great Treasury Raid,* Random House, New York, 1962.

welfare recipients were asked how they felt about being on welfare, most of the mothers on welfare said they felt bothered by it. Over one-half agreed that "getting money from welfare makes a person feel ashamed."[9]

When asked, "Would you prefer to work for pay or stay home?" seven of ten mothers elected to work.[10] Among those who preferred to stay at home, 77% gave "child care" as a reason and 20% offered health reasons.

Eighty % of the Negro mothers preferred to work, in contrast to 60% of the Puerto Ricans and 55% of the whites. Even mothers with preschool children preferred to work. When asked, "If there were a place around to leave the children all day for free, would you rather stay home and take care of the children yourself or work for pay?" about 60% of the mothers with preschool children replied that they would prefer to work.[11]

In Cleveland, when Title V programs offered entry-level positions to AFDC mothers, the number of applicants far exceeded the number of available places. This experience has been repeated whenever entry-level positions, which at least

---

[9] *Families on Welfare in New York City,* Preliminary Report No. 5, Graduate Center, The City University of New York, 1967, p. 10.
[10] *Ibid.,* Preliminary Report No. 3, 1967, p. 7.
[11] *Ibid.,* pp. 7–8.

guarantee their present standard of living, have been offered.

Further, the uneven distribution of youth in AFDC families in Cuyahoga County (72% of the youth are under 12) indicates that mothers are leaving the welfare rolls as their children become older.[12]

MYTH: *Present welfare standards have no effect on a child's education performance.*

A study of a sample of children in AFDC families in 1968 revealed that less than half of the children were in the proper grade for their age. The average deficiency was 1.56 years.[13] While this can be partially traced to the fact that AFDC families move frequently and that some have migrated from areas where schools are poor, the central reasons lie in the lack of positive familial resources, and the excessive tension, apathy, and insecurity typical of the family living under the pressures of an income inadequate for necessities.[14]

The insecurity of family life undermines the sense of personal control by the student whose total environment is suffused by the problems of welfare. This feeling of lack of control in determining his own future or in having a clear and acceptable conception of himself may have a more detrimental effect on his educational performance than any other single factor.[15]

The director of the Cuyahoga County Welfare Department, speaking to the U.S. Congress in 1967, underlined the disadvantages faced by 33,000 AFDC youth in this county. "Daily these youth have to face life with the realization that they have less of a chance to achieve a place in our society because they lack clothing, school books, and even shoes to attend school. Each night many thousands of children go to bed hungry, in housing that is inadequate, that is crawling with roaches, infested with rodents." To the question, "Why aren't they motivated to better themselves?", he responded, "The fact is that it takes so much strength just to barely exist that it would sap the strength of the strongest of us."[16]

---

[12]*Preliminary Study of Characteristics of AFDC Population.*
[13]*Ibid.*
[14]Coleman, *Equality of Educational Opportunity.*
[15]*Ibid.*
[16]Statement of Eugene Burns, Cuyahoga County Welfare Director, before the House Ways and Means Committee, Washington, April 6, 1967.

In the New York City study mentioned above, 30% of the mothers on welfare with children in school said that at times the children stayed home from school because they lacked shoes or clothing; 20% reported that they sometimes kept the children home from school because they were ashamed of the way they were dressed. About 33% reported that they sometimes kept the children from school because the children were needed at home.[17]

MYTH: *The welfare budget in Ohio is adequate for a family to live comfortably.*

The U.S. Commission on Civil Rights, after studying Ohio's payments, said that for most clients the inadequacy of cash payments "results in deficient diets, insufficient clothing, and substandard housing." The payments now average 83 cents a day per person, excluding rent. The total budget of a typical family under the AFDC program in Ohio (mother and three children) is $193 a month. (The state itself sets $232 as the bare minimum for "health and decency.") The money is allocated in the following manner: $70 average for rent, $20 maximum for utilities, and $103 for food, clothing, and household supplies.

If the client has to pay rent above the maximum (which is usually the case) the family must use part of the food allowance or face eviction. During the winter the utility allowance falls short of the actual bill, and utilities are often denied because the full bill cannot be paid.

In 1959, home economists determined the basic minimum standard of expenses for welfare families. This standard was equivalent to a little more than one-half of the U.S. Bureau of Labor Standards' "modest but adequate" budget for a family. Since 1959, grants have been cut even below the state's minimum subsistence level.

Presently, families receiving Aid to Families with Dependent Children are said to be receiving 83% of the minimum subsistence, but even this is misleading. Although the over-all figure is set at 83% of subsistence level, the actual percentage falls even lower. For example, the state sets a maximum figure for rent and utilities and pays that amount according to family

---

[17]*Families on Welfare in New York City,* Preliminary Report No. 7, pp. 2–3.

and apartment size. A family of from four to nine members is allowed $80 a month for rent and $20 a month for heating, lighting, and cooking utilities.

However, if the family pays above the $80 maximum allowance, it must take this money from the already deficient food and clothing budget. Utilities more often than not total much more than $20, especially since most housing available to welfare clients is substandard and costs more than the average to heat.

In essence, the state subsidizes landlords and utility companies at the expense of food and clothing for welfare clients. If the family elects to purchase food or clothing, evictions and cutoff of utility service cause additional crises for the family. Because of the low payments, welfare clients are continually paying premiums on necessities. For example, the gas company offers a 3% discount for payment of its bill before a designated date. Since the highest cost for gas is in the winter when clients often are forced to fall behind, they cannot take advantage of the discount. What this amounts to is subsidization by the poor of the more affluent who have no trouble meeting the bill and receiving the discount.

MYTH: *Clients have children in order to obtain more money from the state.*

The extra payment a mother receives for a child averages about $3.50 a week, hardly enough to make an additional child profitable. Indeed, the economic plight of the family increases in proportion to the number of children, rather than the opposite. For example, a family on welfare with three children would not receive additional rent money unless the family size increased to 10. If the family size increased from three to nine, the state would pay $8 a month more for all utilities.

MYTH: *Ohio can't afford to pay adequate welfare benefits to the poor.*

As a general rule there is a close relationship between welfare expenditures and the financial capacity of state and local governments. Ohio is a tragic exception. While Ohio is among the wealthiest states and the cost of living is one of the highest in the nation, Ohio's expenditures to meet the human needs of its citizens has fallen far short of what is desirable.

In 1960, the state ranked 5th among the 50 states in personal income and 16th in average per capita income; it was 3rd in the value added to goods after manufacture and the 4th wealthiest state in assessed value of property. In 1967, Ohio ranked 19th in expenditures per inhabitant for public assistance, including medical care payments. In 1966, it ranked 29th in payments to needy families with dependent children, with a payment of $33.15 per month per person; in the same year it was 21st in payments to the disabled on public assistance.

APPENDIX C
POVERTY AND UNEMPLOYMENT IN CLEVELAND

(Extracted from the Report of the Council for Economic Opportunity, April, 1968, *Characteristics of Poverty in Cleveland*)

Poverty is a family problem. It affects not only the parents but the children as well. In Cleveland, there are 60,000 children and young adults in poverty households. The problems which these children and young adults must overcome if they are to enter the mainstream of American life are many. These become evident when the social and economic characteristics of the residents of the poverty area are compared with those of the rest of the city.

MALE UNEMPLOYMENT

Male unemployment (Table C.1) in the five target areas is three times greater than in the remainder of Cleveland: 12.4% as compared to 4.2%. While accounting for less than 29% of Cleveland's total labor force, the target areas contain more than 50.9% of its total unemployment. In the Central area the unemployment rate is from four to five times higher than the remainder and is increasing instead of decreasing as in the rest of the city. The special census of 1965 showed that while the unemployment in Glenville had dropped 30% (from 10% to 6.9%) between 1960 and 1965, unemployment had risen in East Central from 13.3% to 15.5%, in West Central from 17.2% to 19%, in Goodrich from 8.5% to 13.6%, in West Side from 7.8% to 9.4%.[1]

---

[1]*Characteristics of Selected Neighborhoods in Cleveland, Ohio*, U.S. Bureau of Census Current Population Reports, Series P.23, No. 21. April, 1965.

FEMALE UNEMPLOYMENT

In 1965, the unemployment rate for females in Cleveland was 8.3% (Table C.1). The incidence of unemployment for females in the target areas was three times as high as the rate for the remainder of Cleveland: 15.4% as compared to 5.3%. While male unemployment decreased slightly between 1960 and 1965, female unemployment in the target areas increased 26.2% (from 12.2% to 15.4%). The data indicates that the unemployment rate for women increased in *every neighborhood* within the target areas: in Glenville 9.3% as compared to 12.4%, in Hough 13.2% as compared to 17.5%, in West Central 13.4% as compared to 24.3%, in East Central 11.0% as compared to 13.9%, in Kinsman 12.9% as compared to 16.4%, and in West Side 9.6% as compared to 11.3%.

The higher and disproportionate rate of female unemployment in the target areas is illustrated by the fact that, while the target areas contain only 29.9% of the total labor force, they contribute 52.0% of the total female unemployment for the City of Cleveland.[2]

MEDIAN FAMILY INCOME

The second measure which reflects, in part, the poverty of the target areas, is the gap between the median income of the target areas' families and that of families in the remainder of Cleveland (Tables C.1 and C.6). In 1965, the median family income in Cleveland was $6,895; outside the target areas the median family income averaged $7,532. Within the target areas, however, it ranged from $3,000 in West Central to $6,156 in Glenville, making the median family income in the target areas between $639 and $3,895 below the city-wide median.

Within the core of the target area, specifically in Central, Kinsman, and Hough, the disparity between the median family income of the area's residents and that of families in the remainder of the city is far greater. Here, in what some commentators have called the "crisis ghetto," the median real income of the area's families actually declined during the period

---

[2]*Ibid.*

between 1960 and 1965, with the gap between the median income of the area's residents and that of those in the rest of the target areas actually increasing. This is shown in the following table:

Median Income

	1960	1965
Crisis ghetto	$3,170–4,900	$3,000–4,160
Rest of target areas	5,446–5,960	5,458–6,156
Average for remainder of city	6,832	7,532

Hence not only had the median family income in the crisis ghetto decreased, but the gap between the highest median income in the crisis ghetto and the lowest in the other target areas had increased from $550 in 1960 to $1,300 by 1965. In addition, the median family income for the rest of the target areas was, in contrast with 1960, further from the average median income for the remainder of Cleveland.[3]

AID TO FAMILIES WITH DEPENDENT CHILDREN

Closely related to the high, and in certain cases increasing, unemployment rate and to the decrease in the median income for the target areas, is the increasing proportion of families receiving assistance from the Aid to Families with Dependent Children program (Table C.5). From 1963 to 1966, the number of AFDC cases in the City of Cleveland rose by over 50%, with 14,671 cases reported in 1966, as compared to 9,728 cases in 1963. Of the 47,912 AFDC recipients in 1967, 36,412 were children; of this total, 87.3% were nonwhite. In 1966, 78.8% of the cases lived in the Central, Glenville, Hough, Kinsman, and Mt. Pleasant areas. In each of these communities, with the exception of Mt. Pleasant, the proportion of families receiving AFDC was 12.5% greater than the city-wide figure. The relative isolation of those on AFDC in the city is emphasized by the fact that only 18% of the total

---

[3]*Ibid.*

cases in the City of Cleveland resided outside of the target areas in 1966.[4]

The information documented above, particularly that revealed by the 1965 special census, suggests a growing polarization between the target areas and the remainder of Cleveland. This information has led some commentators to conclude that two highly separate communities are emerging side by side, with the poor becoming the largest occupant of one, and competitive and upwardly mobile families being gradually isolated in the remainder of Cleveland.

YOUTH IN THE TARGET AREAS

In 1965, there were 335,627 Clevelanders under the age of 22. Of this total, 17.3%, or 58,200, were classified as living in poverty. While the target areas contained only 37.19% of the youth population, they contained over 73% of the youth living in poverty as compared to only 8% in the remainder of the city. In the "crisis ghetto" the concentration of poverty youth is even higher; in Kinsman and East Central the proportion of youth in poverty is 40%; in Hough, where over 13,300 young people live, it is almost 50%; and in West Central nearly 59% are living in poverty. (See Tables C.1 and C.4a–c.)

Between 1960 and 1965 the absolute number of children on poverty increased in all but two of the target areas. Simultaneously, the total number of children in five of the six target areas decreased; thus, within the target areas not only did the number of youth in poverty increase, but the proportion of children on poverty is increasing significantly as well. In Glenville the youth in poverty population increased 4,245, or 61.9%, while the total youth population increased only 22.5%. This represents an increase in the rate of youth poverty from 21.9% in 1960 to 29.1% in 1965. This rate increase is second only to Hough, which rose from 37.4% to 41.2% of the total youth. (See Table C.2.)

The census revealed another important trend (which the earlier AFDC data suggested): that the percentage of poverty

---

[4]"Fact Sheets on Aid to Dependent Children," Welfare Federation of Cleveland, 1960–67.

children living in female-headed homes was rapidly increasing. Approximately 58%, or 34,000, of all youth living in poverty in 1965, as compared to 42.5% in 1960, lived in female-headed homes (see Table C.8). For Negro youths the percentage has increased about 15%, from 49 out of every 100 youths in 1960 to 64 out of every 100 in 1965. Within the target areas the number of Negro children in poverty in female-headed homes has increased phenomenally from 16,812 in 1960 to 26,202 in 1965. For the age groups 6–13, 14–15, and 16–17, the increase has been 71%, 90%, and 63%, respectively.[5]

DROPOUT RATE

Another product of the general economic malaise found in the target areas is the high dropout rate in the schools (Table C.3). The Board of Education follow-up study of three schools in the target areas suggested that, with some variations, the dropout rate was strongly linked to a cycle which included parental unemployment, high sibling dropout, parental separation, and state of public dependency.[6] Another Board study showed that the dropout rate in Title I schools (those in the poverty area) was substantially higher than the dropout rate for the non-Title I schools.[7] The available data on the dropout rate suggests that in the six schools in the target areas, between 40% and 60% of the students that enter the tenth grade, and in certain schools the ninth grade, will not graduate. Of the 4,100 who dropped out of school in 1966–67, no less than 3,300 resided within the target areas. While data do not permit specific comparisons, earlier data, when contrasted with the available data, suggest that the dropout rate for the target areas is increasing.[8] When this high dropout rate is joined with the finding of the Board of Education, that employment opportunities for dropouts are extremely limited (65% unemployed), this situation becomes doubly grave.

---

[5]*Characteristics of Selected Neighborhoods.*

[6]*In Depth Follow-Up of Dropouts from Three Inner-City High Schools,* Bureau of Educational Research, Cleveland Public Schools, January, 1968.

[7]*Report of Dropout Rates,* Cleveland Board of Education, October 16, 1967.

[8]*Ibid.*

JUVENILE DELINQUENCY

One of the most tragic effects of poverty and the pressures of poverty upon family life is reflected in the high male juvenile delinquency rates for the target areas (Table C.9). The rate for the City of Cleveland is 100.6 cases per 1,000 boys, whereas in Glenville and Hough the rate is over 220 per 1,000, and West Central has the highest rate in the City—326.6. (It is significant that West Central also has the lowest median income of any area in the city.) When these rates are compared to the rate for the remainder of the city (76.9 per 1,000), the tremendous impact of poverty upon family life and youth behavior is apparent. Not only are the target area rates much higher than the remainder rates, but they are also rising faster.[9]

YOUTH UNEMPLOYMENT IN SOCIAL PLANNING AREAS

In 1966 the Cleveland Board of Education, conducted a survey of youth between the ages of 16 and 21 in the 12 social planning areas of the inner city[10] (Table C.7, also see Table C.1). This survey found that 4,886 young people between the ages of 16 and 21 were unemployed, or 17.3% of the total youth population in these areas. However, when those in school, in service, and married females were subtracted, the unemployment rate for those in the labor market rose to 53.6%. Within the areas surveyed there was a marked contrast between those areas heavily populated by families in poverty and those with lower percentages of poverty families. In the areas of greatest poverty (Central, East Central, West Central, Hough, Kinsman, and Glenville) the rate of youth unemployment was found to be 64.7%. For the remaining areas (Mt. Pleasant, Norwood, Goodrich, Tremont, and the Near West Side) the rate was 39.8%. These same high-poverty areas have the highest school dropout rates in the city. When this high dropout rate is coupled to the nongraduate unemployment rate of 65%, we begin to see the cumulative effect of family poverty regenerating itself.

---

[9]"Fact Sheets on Juvenile Delinquency," Welfare Federation of Cleveland, 1966.
[10]*In Depth Follow-Up of Dropouts.*

A nationwide survey on youth unemployment conducted by the Department of Labor in 1967,[11] illustrates the severity of youth unemployment in the target areas. Whereas the nationwide survey found the unemployment rate for 16 and 17 year olds to be 14.8%, the rate for the 12 social planning areas was 71%. For 18 and 19 year olds the nationwide rate was 11.3%, whereas for the 12 social planning areas the rate was 51%. Further, while the study found nonwhite unemployment to be between two to two and one-half times higher than white unemployment (with the highest rate appearing among nonwhite females), the nationwide nonwhite unemployment rate was slightly less than two-fifths of the rate for the five highest poverty areas in Cleveland—26.5% as compared to 64.7%.

Seven out of 10 of the unemployed youth are 18 to 20 years of age. Of these, 55% have not held a full-time job and only a quarter of them have taken part in some job training programs. In effect, the Board's study suggests that a large percentage of the young people living in the inner city will not outgrow this unemployment. The survey found that the unemployment rate of 54.7% for 18 through 20 year olds dropped only to 40% for those 21 to 29. Hence for a substantial number of youth in the target areas the pattern is set: The conditions of poverty increase the probabilities of dropping out of school; the bulk of dropouts will enter manhood unemployed, and, for many, lack of steady employment appears to be a reality that they will face throughout their adult lives.

A DESCRIPTION OF THREE TARGET AREAS

Hough. The Hough area has been the starting point for many young Negro families who have moved up economically. It has not, however, been able to retain these families. A quick perusal of the census figures for 1965 shows a marked decline in the number of families with incomes between $4,000 and $9,000. The growing emigration of this population accounts in large extent for the sharp drop of 18% in Hough's population between 1960 and 1965. During the same period the median family income for the area fell by 16%. This is strongly related to the middle-income departure but also to a

---

[11]U.S. Department of Labor, *1967 Handbook of Labor Statistics.*

second important social change: the growth over the five-year period in the absolute number of female-headed families (Table C.8) and the simultaneous deterioration of an already weak female economic situation. The median real income for female-headed families in Hough fell from a shockingly low $2,000 in 1960 to $1,950 in 1965. Female unemployment increased by 40% to 17.5%. As a result, the number of Negro females heading households in poverty has grown by 60% (to 2,541). This is graphically borne out by the rapidly rising AFDC rate for the area. In the period between 1963 and 1966 the AFDC rate rose 51%. In 1966 one out of every five families (204.4 out of every 1,000) was receiving aid to dependent children.[12] As a result of these changes, Hough has been left with an increasing proportion of economically handicapped people.

Over-all, the number of children in poverty in Hough increased 28.9% in the five years after the 1960 census. As of 1965, 13,304, *or nearly half the children of Hough,* lived in poverty; 70% of these children came from female-headed families, as contrasted with 52.8% in 1960. During the same five years the number of children in such families rose 57.3% while *the total number of children in Hough decreased 2.4%.* In 1965, 84% of all children in female-headed homes in Hough were in poverty. This means that 33.4% of the children in the area lived in female-headed homes in a condition of poverty.

As Hough becomes increasingly an area of families in poverty, especially female-headed families, it becomes an increasingly troubled area. The school dropout rate has doubled. The male juvenile delinquency rate is high and its rise is rapidly accelerating. In 1960 there were 136.3 cases of delinquency per every thousand boys; in 1965, 155.6, and in 1966, 220.6.[13] One out of every five boys was delinquent in 1966.

To escape deepening poverty, the young people of Hough must gain employable skills through education and training. Evidence suggests that they are not gaining these skills presently: 20% of the total high school enrollment drops out of school every year, with approximately 40% of those now in the tenth grade in area schools dropping out before graduation. Even for graduates of the area high schools, the past rate of employment has not been encouraging. In point of fact the

---

[12]"Fact Sheets on Aid to Dependent Children," 1960–67.
[13]"Fact Sheets on Juvenile Delinquency," 1960–66.

1966 school board survey found that the graduate unemployment rate in the area was 59% compared to a general area-youth unemployment rate of 60%.[14] The equally disadvantageous employment prospects for high school graduates suggests that youth in the area may see little value in remaining in school.

Glenville. At first glance, the over-all conditions in Glenville appear to be improving. Unlike most of the remainder of the target areas, the median income for this area is rising and male unemployment has declined noticeably, from 10.7% to 7.0%. This increasing prosperity is of less relevance, however, to a particular segment of the population—the Negro female-headed household. Negro female unemployment has risen 20% to 12.5%; the number of female-headed families in poverty *doubled* from 1,118 in 1959 to 2,154 in 1965; and the rate over a four-year period of Aid to Families with Dependent Children has risen dramatically (80%). A major ramification of this change is the more than doubling (61.9%) of the number of youth in poverty; 4,245 more children were in poverty in 1965 than in 1960. Children from female-headed families provided the overwhelming bulk of this increase. In this category the increase was *140%* (from 2,965 to 7,137).

One serious consequence of this growth was suggested by a Board of Education survey which showed that 42% of the dropouts in Glenville came from single-parent families.[15] As of 1965, 58.4% of poverty youth were in female-headed homes. In Glenville, 64.2% of all poverty youth come from nonwhite single-parent, female-headed homes. The change in the male juvenile delinquency rate has been even more radical in Glenville than in Hough. In 1960 Glenville had a delinquency rate of 119.6 per 1,000 boys; by 1966 the rate had risen to 234.7.

While the over-all conditions of Glenville are admittedly different from Hough, certain difficulties of the latter are repeated in the former: a growing number of broken homes, with mothers who lack employable skills finding it extremely difficult to provide for their families on a decreasing real income. To a large extent, the conditions of poverty seem to generate their own reinforcements. Too often children subject

---

[14] *In Depth Follow-Up of Dropouts.*
[15] *Ibid.*

to the tremendous and debilitating pressures of poverty fail to acquire the necessary skills, education, and opportunities to escape this cycle. Having failed in this, they are prone to delinquency, dropping out, and marginal employment.

Near West Side. The Near West Side is an old inner-city neighborhood composed of traditionally ethnic enclaves and more recently infused with large Puerto Rican and Appalachian immigrations.

Data provided by the Board of Education's study of mobility and immigration,[16] which emphasizes the high population instability in the area, suggests patterns which are reminiscent of the Hough area 10 years ago. Of the five city elementary schools with a turnover of greater than 50%, *three* are in the Near West Side; of the five city junior high schools showing a residential change greater than 20%, three are in the Near West Side. The high school in the Near West Side was one of the three city senior high schools with a mobility and immigration rate greater than 20%. To a large extent these figures reflect the large influx of poorer Appalachian whites and Puerto Ricans and the exiting of the younger working class families to the fringes of Cleveland and the suburbs.

West High School has the highest dropout rate of all city senior high schools. Over 50% of the students enrolled in the tenth grade at West High will not graduate, with an average of 22.9% of the total student enrollment dropping out each year. This compares to the city-wide dropout rate of 13.1%.

A follow-up survey on recent dropouts conducted by the Board of Education indicated the depth of poverty in the area and the persistent relationship between poverty and dropping out of school[17]; 42.5% of the dropouts are from families with unemployed parents; 46.7% of the parents were unskilled workers, and 85.7% did not graduate from high school. Similarly, 76.2% of the older siblings of the dropouts were themselves school dropouts. Lastly, the fact that a substantial number of dropouts were not seeking employment suggests that lack of education, lack of skills, and frequent lack of employment is an expected condition of life for a large number of Near West Side residents.

---

[16]*Study of Mobility and Migration in Cleveland Public Schools, 1966–1967,* Bureau of Educational Research, Cleveland Public Schools.
[17]*In Depth Follow-Up of Dropouts.*

Table C.1. A Profile of Social Characteristics for Target Areas

	CLEVELAND TOTAL	GLENVILLE	HOUGH	WEST CENTRAL	EAST CENTRAL	KINSMAN	WEST SIDE	GOOD-RICH	REMAINDER OF CLEVELAND
Total population[a]	810,858	85,441	58,979	21,442	39,564	14,841	27,059	15,578	547,954
Negro[a]	276,376	79,913	51,861	17,317	38,053	12,267	598	1,494	74,873
% Negro	34.08	93.5	87.9	80.7	96.2	82.7	2.2	9.6	13.7
Unemployment in labor force[a]									
Males	12,970	1,332	1,601	720	1,374	322	598	645	6,378
% Male	6.4	6.9	13.4	14.0	15.5	11.2	9.4	13.8	4.4
Females	9,660	1,637	1,332	547	759	250	341	159	4,635
% Female	8.3	12.4	17.5	24.3	13.9	16.4	11.3	8.1	5.6
Median income[a]	6,895	6,156	4,050	3,000	8,857	4,164	5,458	5,883	7,532
Aid to dependent children[b]									
Number of cases	14,671	3,305	3,767	1,083	1,947	768	1,031	120	2,650
Rate per 1,000 units	55.0	138.1	204.4	151.3	135.6	136.7	44.2	28.3	16.7
Total youth population under 21[a]	335,627	38,127	27,612	9,284	15,675	6,987	10,918	4,915	192,285
Total youth in poverty	58,022	11,106	13,004	4,961	6,374	3,119	2,977	789	15,692
% Youth in poverty	17.3	29.1	48.2	53.4	40.7	44.6	27.3	16.1	8.2
% Youth in poverty in female-headed homes	58.35	65.3	70.9	57.8	55.4	60.4	37.8	41.1	48.9
Male juvenile delinquency rate per 1,000 males 12–17[b]	100.6	234.7	220.6	326.6	174.0	164.8	100.3	86.4	76.9
Number of youth 16–21[c]	51,871	6,075	4,326	1,758	2,559	1,218	4,624	798	30,563
Number unemployed[d]	4,886[e]	905	1,097	241	778	151	541	140	
% Unemployed	17.3[e]	14.9	25.9	13.7	27.5	12.4	11.7	17.5	
% In labor market unemployed	53.6[e]	57.0	66.6	52.0	70.5	50.0	46.0	42.0	

[a]U.S. Special Census for Cleveland, 1965, Series P. 23, No. 21.
[b]Welfare Federation of Cleveland Fact Sheet for 1966.
[c]Cleveland Board of Education, "Unemployed Out of School Youth Survey," 1966.
[d]The Board study was limited to the 12 social planning areas of the inner city; totals refer only to the 12 social planning areas.
[e]Data do *not* include information for the remainder of Cleveland.

Table C.2. Youth Population of City of Cleveland, by Age, Race, and Poverty Level

	1960				1965			
	CITY	WHITE	NEGRO	% NEGRO	CITY	WHITE	NEGRO	% NEGRO
Total population	876,050	623,020	250,889	28.63	810,858	531,506	276,376	34.08
Youth Population								
Total (under 21)	330,389	219,791	110,498	33.5	335,627	203,518	132,082	39.4
Under 5	101,139	64,660	36,499	36.1	88,311	53,537	34,847	39.5
5–9	82,916	51,948	30,932	37.3	88,836	51,364	37,472	42.4
10–14	64,440	46,373	22,067	32.2	72,438	40,961	31,477	43.5
15–19	54,378	35,589	14,789	27.2	63,565	41,508	22,057	34.7
20–21	23,416	17,205	6,211	26.6	22,477	16,248	6,229	27.7
% of total population	37.7	35.3	44.04		41.4	38.3	47.8	
Poverty Youth								
Total	56,869	20,786	36,083	36.4	58,020	15,328	42,692	73.6
Under 5	19,971	7,038	12,933	64.8	16,985	4,447	12,538	73.8
5–9	16,513	5,983	10,530	63.8	16,919	4,218	12,692	75.1
10–14	13,172	4,894	8,278	62.8	15,047	3,789	11,258	74.8
15–19	5,898	2,370	3,528	59.8	7,779	2,522	5,257	67.6
20–21	1,315	501	814	61.9	1,299	352	947	72.9
% Youth in poverty	17.2	9.5	32.7		17.3	7.5	32.3	
Poverty youth in female-headed homes	24,174	6,488	17,686		33,857	6,965	26,892	
% of poverty youth in female-headed homes	42.5	31.2	49.0		58.4	45.4	63.9	

SOURCE: Age and race characteristics for selected neighborhoods are from U.S. Special Census for Cleveland, 1965, Series P. 23, No. 21; poverty data interpolated.

Table C.3. Comparison of Annual Dropout Rates in Non-Title I and Title I Senior High Schools

SCHOOL	GRADE 10	GRADE 11	GRADE 12	TOTAL[a]
Non-Title I				
John Adams	16.7%	15.8%	7.8%	13.6%
John F. Kennedy	13.4	12.8	6.5	11.2
South High	7.6	13.2	5.3	8.7
West Technical	9.5	10.4	5.9	8.6
John Marshall	7.4	8.6	6.7	7.5
Collinwood	7.2	8.8	4.9	6.8
James F. Rhodes	5.1	7.9	6.1	6.3
Non-title I dropout rate	10.2%	11.2%	6.2%	
Title I				
West High	29.3%	22.4%	13.6%	22.9%
East High	28.0	19.4	10.2	21.5
John Hay	23.6	21.4	11.9	19.8
East Technical	20.7	20.8	14.4	18.9
Thomas A. Edison[a]	18.3	18.3	17.4	18.0
Lincoln	22.4	15.6	9.3	16.0
Glenville	13.5	17.5	10.3	13.9
Max S. Hayes	9.1	10.8	13.8	11.3
Jane Addams	11.7	13.0	4.6	9.7
Title I dropout rate	20.2%	18.5%	11.7%	
Total dropout rate	15.6%	14.5%	8.8%	13.1%

[a] Ungraded school figures prorated over a three-year period.

SOURCE: Board of Education Report of Dropout Rates, October 16, 1967.

Table C.4a. Youth, by Age and Poverty Level, for Kinsman and East Central Target Areas

	Kinsman Area			East Central Area		
	1965	1960	PER CENT CHANGE	1965	1960	PER CENT CHANGE
Total youth	6,987	7,869	−11.2	15,675	17,585	−10.9
Under 6	2,691	3,536		4,500	6,851	
6–13	2,923	3,111		7,535	7,256	
14–15	541	372		1,524	1,160	
16–17	401	398		1,040	932	
18–21	431	542		1,076	1,386	
Poverty youth total	3,119	2,796	−11.55	6,774	7,215	−6.0
Under 6	1,289	1,448		2,093	3,038	
6–13	1,314	983		2,975	2,956	
14–15	220	131		544	443	
16–17	144	117		435	331	
18–21	152	117		327	447	
% of total youth in poverty	44.6	35.5	+25.6	40.7	43.2	−5.8
Poverty youth in non-white female-headed homes	1,884	1,106		3,531	3,386	
% of total poverty youth	59.1	39.6	+49.2	55.4	46.9	+18.1

SOURCE: U.S. Special Census for Cleveland, 1965, Series P. 23, No. 21.

Table C.4b. Youth, by Age and Poverty Level, for Hough and Glenville Target Areas

	Hough Area			Glenville Area		
	1965	1960	PER CENT CHANGE	1965	1960	PER CENT CHANGE
Total youth	27,612	28,290	−2.4	38,127	31,238	+22.5
Under 6	9,569	13,178		13,414	13,074	
6–13	11,974	10,591		16,405	12,454	
14–15	2,316	1,397		3,268	1,664	
16–17	1,972	1,460		2,601	1,871	
18–21	1,781	1,664		2,439	2,175	
Poverty youth total	13,304	10,588	+25.7	11,106	6,861	+61.9
Under 6	4,924	5,317		4,618	3,164	
6–13	5,892	3,951		4,894	2,787	
14–15	954	473		732	293	
16–17	674	437		504	347	
18–21	560	407		358	265	
% of total youth in poverty	42.8	37.4	+28.9	29.1	21.9	+32.8
Poverty youth in non-white female-headed homes	9,124	5,086		7,137	2,965	
% of total poverty youth	68.5	48.0	+42.7	64.2	43.2	+48.9

SOURCE: U.S. Special Census for Cleveland, 1965, Series P. 23, No. 21.

Table C.4c. Youth, by Age and Poverty Level, for Near West Side and West Central Target Areas

	NEAR WEST SIDE AREA			WEST CENTRAL AREA		
	1965	1960	PER CENT CHANGE	1965	1960	PER CENT CHANGE
Total youth	10,918	11,553	−5.5	9,284	13,401	−30.8
Under 6	4,015	4,655		2,916	4,960	
6–13	4,651	4,552		4,108	5,479	
14–15	925	783		805	877	
16–17	756	762		716	701	
18–21	571	801		739	884	
Poverty youth total	2,977	2,897	+2.7	4,961	7,553	−35.4
Under 6	1,175	1,263		1,634	2,453	
6–13	1,320	1,166		2,218	3,279	
14–15	257	198		417	494	
16–17	169	175		364	399	
18–21	56	45		328	428	
% of total youth	27.3	25.1	+8.7	53.4	56.4	−5.3
Poverty youth in non-white female-headed homes	1,124	917		2,869	3,933	
% of total poverty youth	37.8	31.6	+19.6	57.8	52.2	+10.6

SOURCE: U.S. Special Census for Cleveland, 1965, Series P. 23, No. 21.

Table C.5. Aid to Families with Dependent Children, City of Cleveland, for Selected Neighborhoods

AREA	1963		1966		PER CENT INCREASE (CHANGE IN RATE)	INCREASE	
	NO.	RATE[a]	NO.	RATE[a]		NO.	PER CENT
Central	657	119.8	834	156.1	30.3	177	26.9
East Central	799	80.4	1,113	115.1	43.2	314	39.3
West Central	961	113.9	1,083	151.3	32.8	122	12.7
Glenville	1,851	76.7	3,305	138.1	80.0	1,454	78.5
Hough	2,796	135.4	3,767	204.4	51.0	971	34.7
Kinsman	513	90.8	768	136.7	50.0	255	49.7
Near West Side	600	30.1	693	38.2	8.1	93	13.5
Total	8,177	92.4	11,563	134.2	51.5%	3,386	41.4%
Cleveland City Total	9,728	36.0	14,671	55.0	14.0%	5,732	58.9%

[a] Per 1,000 occupied family units.
SOURCE: Welfare Federation of Cleveland Fact Sheets for 1963 and 1966.

Table C.6. Median Incomes of Nonwhite Families in Selected Areas

AREA	1960	1965	DIFFERENCE	PER CENT CHANGE	DEVIATION FROM CITY MEAN	
					1960	1965
Glenville	5,814	6,117	+303	+5.2	−511 (8.1%)	−778 (11.29%)
Hough	4,732	3,966	−766	−16.2	−1,593 (25.19%)	−2,929 (42.5%)
West Central	3,210	2,984	−226	−7.1	−3,115 (49.25%)	−3,911 (56.7%)
East Central	4,216	3,887	−329	−7.8	−2,109 (33.34%)	−3,008 (43.6%)
Kinsman	4,346	3,729	−617	−28.4	−1,979 (31.29%)	−3,166 (45.9%)
Mt. Pleasant	4,742	6,513	+1,771	+37.3	−1,583 (25.03%)	−382 (5.5%)
City of Cleveland (all families)	6,325	6,895	+570	+9.0		

SOURCE: U.S. Special Census for Cleveland, 1965, Series P. 23, No. 21.

Table C.7. Status of Youth, 16-21, in Selected Social Planning Areas, 1966 (Estimated)

AREA	TOTAL 16-21 YOUTHS	IN SCHOOL NO.	%	OUT OF SCHOOL EMPLOYED NO.	%	UNEMPLOYED NO.	%	YOUTH IN LABOR FORCE NO.	%	UNEMPLOYED IN LABOR FORCE %
East Central	1,663	562	33.8	239	14.4	587	35.3	826	49.7	72.0
Central	936	553	59.1	85	9.1	192	20.4	276	29.5	69.0
West Central	1,758	1,192	67.8	211	12.0	241	13.7	452	25.7	52.0
Glenville	6,075	4,082	67.2	686	11.3	905	14.9	1,591	26.2	57.0
Goodrich	798	439	55.0	199	25.0	140	17.5	339	42.5	42.0
Hough	4,236	2,190	51.7	551	13.0	1,097	25.9	2,052	38.9	66.6
Kinsman	1,218	820	67.3	151	12.4	151	12.4	302	24.8	50.0
Mt. Pleasant	2,574	1,416	55.0	512	19.9	443	17.2	955	37.1	46.6
Near West Side	4,624	2,520	54.5	883	19.1	541	11.7	1,424	30.8	46.0
North Broadway	1,163	694	59.7	191	16.4	70	6.0	259	22.4	27.0
Norwood	1,617	946	58.5	236	14.6	212	13.1	448	29.7	47.3
Tremont	1,585	751	47.4	376	23.7	242	15.3	619	39.0	39.3
Total	28,247	16,165	57.2	4,320	15.0	4,821	17.3	9,141	32.3	53.6

NOTE: The unemployment rate for Central, Hough, Kinsman, and Glenville areas = 64.7; the unemployment rate for Mt. Pleasant, Norwood, Goodrich, Tremont, Near West Side, and North Broadway = 39.8.
SOURCE: U.S. Special Census for Cleveland, 1965, Series P. 23, No. 21; Cleveland Board of Education, "Unemployed Out of School Youth Survey," 1966.

Table C.8. Incidence of Poverty Among Negro Female-Headed Households, 1959 and 1964, by Selected Target Areas

	1959		1964	
	POVERTY FAMILIES		POVERTY FAMILIES	
AREA	NO.	%	NO.	%
West Central	1,174	47.6	928	52.6
East Central	1,398	41.9	1,366	51.8
Glenville	1,118	43.0	2,159	55.3
Hough	1,681	48.4	2,541	62.1
Kinsman	360	36.1	532	49.3
Mt. Pleasant	339	38.4	662	54.8
Total	6,070	41.8	8,188	54.3

SOURCE: U.S. Special Census for Cleveland, 1965, Series P. 23, No. 21.

Table C.9. Male Juvenile Delinquency, Ages 12–17, by Selected Target Areas
Rate per 1,000 Boys

AREA	1960	1965	1966	RATE INCREASE (PER CENT)
Central	161.8	194.3	171.8	6.2
East Central	161.9	131.6	176.3	8.9
West Central	160.9	131.2	326.6	102.9
Glenville	119.6	117.1	234.7	96.2
Hough	136.3	115.6	220.6	61.8
Kinsman	112.4	112.3	164.8	46.6
Near West Side	83.1	91.1	113.0	34.8
Mt. Pleasant	66.8	138.2	188.0	181.4
Cleveland average	76.7	86.5	100.6	31.1

SOURCE: Welfare Federation of Cleveland.

APPENDIX D
NATIONAL EXPENDITURES FOR PUBLIC ASSISTANCE FROM STATE AND LOCAL FUNDS, FISCAL YEAR 1967

Table D.1. National Expenditures for Public Assistance from State and Local Funds

STATE	RANK BY PER CAPITA INCOME, 1966	AMOUNT PER $1,000 OF PERSONAL INCOME, 1966	AMOUNT PER INHABITANT, 1967	RANK BY AMOUNT PER INHABITANT
National average		$ 5.40	$15.70	
California	7	$11.45	$38.80	1
New York	6	10.35	36.00	2
Oklahoma	37	9.30	22.75	3
Colorado	21	7.85	22.60	4
Massachusetts	10	7.75	22.25	5
Rhode Island	17	6.50	19.75	6
Washington	12	5.50	17.40	7
Minnesota	24	5.95	17.25	8
Connecticut	2	4.25	15.45	9
Michigan	11	4.60	14.75	10
Illinois	3	4.05	14.10	11
Hawaii	14	4.65	14.00	12
Maryland	13	4.45	13.95	13
Kansas	25	4.70	13.45	14
Pennsylvania	20	4.50	13.30	15
Louisiana	43	5.85	13.15	16
Montana	29	4.70	12.40	17
New Jersey	8	3.50	11.85	18
OHIO	16	3.75	11.30	19
Wisconsin	19	3.80	11.25	20
Oregon	22	3.90	11.20	21
Iowa	18	3.70	11.15	22
District of Columbia	1	2.85	11.15	23
Missouri	26	3.95	11.10	24
North Dakota	41	4.35	10.40	25
Alaska	9	3.05	10.10	26
New Hampshire	27	3.60	10.05	27
Wyoming	28	3.55	9.85	28
South Dakota	39	3.80	9.30	29
Arkansas	50	4.65	9.25	30
Vermont	32	3.55	9.15	31

Table D.1. (con't)

STATE	RANK BY PER CAPITA INCOME, 1966	AMOUNT PER $1,000 OF PERSONAL INCOME, 1966	AMOUNT PER INHABITANT, 1967	RANK BY AMOUNT PER INHABITANT
Maine	36	3.45	8.55	32
New Mexico	40	3.40	8.15	33
Utah	35	3.30	8.05	34
Kentucky	45	3.40	7.60	35
Alabama	48	3.60	7.40	36
Nebraska	23	2.50	7.30	37
Nevada	5	2.15	7.30	38
Delaware	4	2.10	7.30	39
Idaho	38	2.80	6.90	40
West Virginia	47	3.00	6.60	41
Texas	34	2.45	6.10	42
Georgia	42	2.40	5.70	43
North Carolina	44	2.35	5.30	44
Tennessee	46	2.30	5.05	45
Arizona	33	2.00	5.00	46
Mississippi	51	2.55	4.50	47
Florida	30	1.75	4.45	48
Indiana	15	1.40	4.30	49
Virginia	31	1.05	2.65	50
South Carolina	49	1.25	2.55	51

SOURCE: Department of Health, Education, and Welfare, *Welfare in Review,* January–February, 1968.

APPENDIX E
SHARE OF COST OF PUBLIC ASSISTANCE PROGRAMS BY LEVELS OF GOVERNMENT

Public assistance is financed by the combined funds of various levels of government with financial participation varying by program category. As an example of programs operated in Cuyahoga County, the following financial contribution by level of government is presented.[1]

For Aid to Families with Dependent Children: 68.9% from federal sources; 25.5% from the state; 4.6% from local communities; and 1.0% from public utilities taxes.

For Aid to Aged: 59.5% from the federal government; 38.7% from the state; and 1.4% from local communities.

For Aid to Disabled: 60.9% from the federal government; 29.1% from the state; 1.4% from local communities; and 8.6% from public utilities taxes.

For Aid for the Blind: 53.7% from the federal government; 40.6% from the state; and 5.7% from local communities.

For General Relief: 41.6% from the state; 41.5% from public utilities taxes; and 16.9% from local sources. (The federal government does not participate in the financing of General Relief.)

---

[1]*Progress in Welfare,* Report of the Ohio Department of Public Welfare, April, 1967, pp. 8–14.

APPENDIX F
TABLES OF STANDARD ALLOWANCES FOR FOOD, CLOTHING, PERSONAL EXPENSES, HOUSING, AND UTILITIES

Table F.1. Standard Allowances to Cover Food, Clothing, and Personal Expenses, Effective July 1, 1967

Aid to Families with Dependent Children (AFDC), Title V, and General Relief

CHILDREN IN ASSISTANCE PLAN[a]	STATE AFDC STANDARD ALLOWANCE	100% STANDARD	DIFFERENCE BETWEEN 100% AND STATE ALLOWANCE: TITLE V	GENERAL RELIEF
1	$ 32	$ 35	$ 3	$ 29
2	60	83	23	52
3	78	107	29	67
4	103	142	39	88
5	127	176	49	109
6	147	204	57	126
7	171	237	66	148
8	195	271	76	170

Standard Allowances in Adult Categories

		STATE STANDARD ALLOWANCE		
	100% STANDARD	AFA (AID FOR THE AGED)	AB (AID FOR THE BLIND)	AFD (AID FOR THE DISABLED)
Size:				
Alone	$60	$60	$60	$50
One other	56	56	56	46
Three or more	53	53	53	42
Restaurant or meals-on-wheels:				
All meals		69	69	69
Principal meals		64	64	64

Standard Allowances in Adult Categories (con't)

	100% STANDARD	STATE STANDARD ALLOWANCE		
		AFA (AID FOR THE AGED)	AB (AID FOR THE BLIND)	AFD (AID FOR THE DISABLED)
Special diets (AFA) (See Manual, Section 461.2)				
Recipient with dependent spouse		99	99	80
Recipient, dependent spouse, with others in household		90	90	72
Personal allowance under board and room arrangement or board and room furnished		15	15	8
Personal allowance in nursing or rest home:				
Ambulatory		8	8	8
Bedfast		5	5	5
Nonrecipient adult		56	56	56

[a]For each additional person add $24. Nonrecipient child allowance = $35.

Table F.2. Maximum Allowance for Housing, Including Utilities (Class I Counties)

PERSONS IN HOUSEHOLD[a]	NUMBER OF ROOMS						
	1	2	3	4	5	6	7
1	$50	$55					
2	50	60	$70	$75			
3	50	60	70	75	$80		
4	55	65	75	80	85	$90	
5	55	65	75	80	85	90	
6	55	65	75	80	90	95	
7	55	65	75	80	90	95	$100
8	55	65	75	80	90	95	100
9	55	65	75	80	90	95	100

[a]For 10 or more add $25 per person to maximum if seven or more rooms.

Table F.3. Allowances for Utilities When not Included in Rent

PERSONS IN HOUSEHOLD	HEAT	LIGHT	COOKING	ALL UTILITIES
1	$ 5	$3	$2	$10
2	7	4	3	14
3	9	4	4	17
4	11	5	4	20
5	12	5	4	21
6	13	5	5	23
7	14	5	5	24
8	15	5	5	25
9 or more	15	5	5	25

APPENDIX G
SOME CASELOAD DATA ON PUBLIC WELFARE IN CUYAHOGA COUNTY

Nearly 10,000 families left the welfare rolls of the Cuyahoga County Welfare Department in 1967. In spite of this, the over-all welfare caseload did not decrease because 13,000 cases were newly opened during the year. AFDC cases reached an *all-time high* in this county during the year. Fatherless families receiving help from this federally assisted program totaled 13,099 by the end of the year.

The following statistics were compiled for the Mayor's Commission on the Crisis in Welfare by Steven A. Minter, Director of Research, Cuyahoga County Welfare Department.

Table G.1. Caseload, Cuyahoga County Welfare Department, 1967

PROGRAM	NEW CASES	CASES CLOSED	TOTAL
Aid to dependent children	3,229	1,705	13,099
Aid to dependent children of the unemployed	540	514	953
Aid to blind	31	28	298
Aid for aged	1,071	970	8,198
Aid to disabled	756	523	3,007
General relief	7,253	5,896	5,754
Total	12,800	9,726	31,309
Vendor payments to clients (AFA, AFD, AB) in nursing homes			1,727
Total caseload			33,036
Number of People on Public Assistance (December, 1967)			
Total adults, federal categories			27,536
Total children, federal categories			48,293
Total			75,829

Table G.2. Growth of AFDC Program, 1957–67

	TOTAL CASES AT END OF YEAR
1957	3,192
1962	7,512
1966	10,864
1967	13,099

Table G.3. Expenditures of Cuyahoga County Welfare Department, 1967

Expenditures for Public Assistance (Income Maintenance)

Total annual expenditures (all programs)		$40,001,382
Aid to dependent children	$21,695,654	
Aid to dependent children of unemployed fathers	2,188,573	
Aid to blind	317,499	
Aid to aged	7,867,731	
Aid to disabled	3,027,356	
General relief	4,904,569	

Expenditures for Supplementation (Local Funds)

General relief supplementation (includes temporary assistance, emergency food orders, utility bill payment, rent orders, household furnishings, emergency clothing)	$ 1,237,393
Duplication of lost or stolen checks	147,130
Housing (emergency lodging, food, Salvation Army, etc.)	174,907
School clothing allowance (September, 1967)	171,985
Special services (guardianship bonds, vital statistics fees, probate court fees, school lunches, and tuition)	147,858
Transportation (Cleveland Transit System, cab vouchers, moving, Greyhound bus fares)	176,361
Total	$ 2,055,634

Other Expenditures Administered by the Welfare Department

Medical bills paid for clients and indigent people (estimated annual total, paid directly by the state)	$20,000,000
Food stamp bonus	$ 4,865,106
Total expenditures in county	$46,922,122

APPENDIX H
NOTE ON ILLEGITIMACY

In commenting on the issue of illegitimacy, the *Report of the National Advisory Commission on Civil Disorders* noted the following:

> The rate of illegitimacy among nonwhite women is closely related to low income and high unemployment. In Washington, D.C., for example, an analysis of 1960 census tracts shows that in tracts with unemployment rates of 12 percent or more among nonwhite men, illegitimacy was over 40 percent. But in tracts with unemployment rates of 2.9 percent and below among nonwhite men, reported illegitimacy was under 20 percent. A similar contrast existed between tracts in which median nonwhite income was under $4,000 (where illegitimacy was 38 percent) and those in which it was $8,000 and over (where illegitimacy was 11 percent).[1]

An examination of the family characteristics of 216 randomly selected families in Cuyahoga County indicated that in 45% of the families there were no out-of-wedlock children, in 28% of the families all the children were out of wedlock, and in 27% there were both in-wedlock and out-of-wedlock children. Of all children in the special survey, 41.7% were born out of wedlock. In 68.8% of all families coming on the AFDC rolls in Cuyahoga County in 1967, illegitimacy was not the significant factor in determining eligibility.

---

[1]*Report of the National Advisory Commission on Civil Disorders,* Washington, 1968, p. 130.

APPENDIX I
FACT SHEET—ISSUE 6—CUYAHOGA COUNTY WELFARE DEPARTMENT, 1968

Amount of levy: 3 mills per $1.00 of assessed valuation (2 mills renewal and 1 mill increase) Cost to taxpayer is $3.00 per $1,000 of assessed property valuation per year.

The Board of County Commissioners has adopted a resolution to submit to the county electorate at the Primary Election on May 7, 1968, a 3 mill levy to help finance the County's share of health, welfare, and relief. The levy will be effective for four (4) years beginning January 1, 1969, through December 31, 1972.

The county health, welfare, and relief program for 1968 is estimated at $99,373,854 and represents an increase of $18,457,457 over 1967 expenditures of $80,916,397. It is now estimated that the Federal and State Governments will provide $69,215,606, leaving a total of $30,158,248 to be raised locally.

The County's share is derived from two sources: 1) two welfare levies; one for 2 mills, and 1 for 1.6 mills; 2) the County General Fund. The combined levies of 3.6 mills will produce approximately $23,047,787 in 1968 and the County General Fund will supplement this figure in the amount of $2,512,000. The remaining portion of the local share is derived from municipalities and miscellaneous receipts and reimbursements. The 1.6 mill levy expires on December 31, 1970. The 2 mill levy expires on December 31, 1968.

The Board of County Commissioners is submitting a 3 mill levy to the county electorate on May 7, 1968, representing a renewal of the present 2 mill authority, plus an increase of 1.0 mill for the years 1969, 1970, 1971, and 1972. Based on a $6,400,000,000 tax duplicate, the 2 mill levy produces $12,800,000. The 1.0 mill increase would produce an additional $6,400,000. The 1.0 mill represents an increase of $1 in taxes for each $1,000 of assessed property valuation. As an example, a home worth $15,000 and appraised at 40% of its value would be assessed for tax purposes at $6,000. The increased taxes on this home would amount to $6 per year.

New laws and standards enacted by the 107th General Assembly require the shifting of more financial and administrative responsibility for welfare from the State to the County level. These laws require 1) the creation of a County Board of Mental Retardation; 2) the creation of a County Mental Health and Retardation Board; 3) that, in order to receive any State matching funds for increasing Aid to Dependent Children grants from the present 83% of state standards, the County must match each State dollar with two County dollars; and 4) an increase of 15% in the annual salaries of County Welfare employees.

The total estimated cost to the County of the foregoing new welfare obligations is approximately $7,350,000. Since the 1 mill increase would produce approximately $6,400,000 in additional funds based on the present tax duplicate, it is quite obvious that all of the welfare demands embodied in the new laws cannot be fulfilled.

This situation, coupled with the fact that the normal County share of health and welfare costs has increased on the average of approximately $1,800,000 per year for the past three years, will lead to the conclusion that the 1 mill increase falls far short of the amount needed to satisfy local demands. The continuing upward spiral of the wages and prices in other fields, such as the Child Welfare Division, County Hospitals, and the County Nursing Home and Clinics, will add to the severity of the financial pinch in the County Budget.

As of December 31, 1967, there are 87,786 people on County welfare programs as follows: Aid for Aged—8,156, Aid for the Blind—299, Aid for the Disabled—3,037, Aid to Dependent Children—60,455, General Relief—15,839. It is estimated that there are more than 50,000 children on the welfare rolls and approximately 4,000 employable out of 87,786. Many of the employables are unskilled, untrained, uneducated, and need concentrated rehabilitative service.

If the 3 mill levy should fail, it would mean that the County would lose the 2 mill authority it now has. This would result in a loss of $12,800,000 annually and also jeopardize the receipt of State and Federal matching funds. Such a condition would also compel drastic retrenchment in all county programs since the County General Fund could not absorb any of this loss.

The 107th General Assembly also enacted new laws imposing additional financial obligations upon the County relating to providing group insurance hospitalization for all County employees, creation of four new Common Pleas judgeships, an increase in the amount of compensation paid to precinct officials at special and primary elections, the total cost of which is now estimated at $2,320,000 in additional demands upon the County General Fund.

APPENDIX J
EXCERPT FROM MEMORANDUM ON PRESUMPTIVE ELIGIBILITY AND WELFARE ASSISTANCE,
by Professor Nathan D. Grundstein

Presumptive eligibility with reference to two classes of welfare assistance:
1. Presumptive eligibility for the Federal (categorical) Relief Programs.
2. Presumptive eligibility for general relief.

Presumptive eligibility in present administrative practices:
1. The practice of presumptive eligibility applies to all categorical relief programs.
2. With reference to general relief, the practice of presumptive eligibility is as follows:
   A. Procedures permit the practice of presumptive eligibility to meet immediate emergency needs at the time of initial contact at the point of welfare intake.

   The work load at intake ranges from 200 to 250 cases per week. There is an uneven distribution of work load over the week. The case load is heaviest on Monday, but while Friday has the lowest number of initial contacts, it is the highest in number of problems presented by clients.

   As of March 25, 1968, the estimate of the number of emergency assistance interviews at the point of initial contact is 3 to 5 per day.

   The Welfare Department keeps a monthly total of all emergency assistance cases.

   B. Procedures permit the practice of presumptive eligibility to meet immediate emergency needs at the time of the first full interview.

   The time lapse between the point of initial contact and the first full interview ranges from 2 to 5 days.

As of March 25, 1968 the estimate of the number of applicants who are granted emergency relief at the point of first full interview is in the range of 50%.

The grant of emergency relief is dependent upon the judgment of the case worker and the case supervisor, since the information requested of the applicant in a sworn statement has not yet been fully verified.

C. For the period from February 26th to March 15th of 1968 the Department of Welfare applied the practice of absolute presumptive eligibility at the point of first full interview.

The above practice was followed for three weeks while the staff of the department devoted full attention to determinations of eligibility.

As of March 25th, the Department had no summary data for this period.

3. Thus, with reference to general relief the Department has had experience with two types of presumptive eligibility practices.

A. Qualified presumptive eligibility.

This is an administrative practice intended to provide for the immediate emergency needs of the welfare applicant. There must be some indication of emergency need on the part of the applicant. There is an element of judgment about the existence of these emergency needs on the part of the caseworker and the case supervisor. Once these needs are judged to exist, emergency relief assistance is granted prior to a final determination of eligibility and without the verification required in non-emergency cases. Emergency assistance includes (a) Food stamps, (b) payment of utility bills, (c) payment of rent, (d) placement on the general relief list.

B. Absolute presumptive eligibility.

This is an administrative practice applied to those welfare applicants who survived the screening for eligibility at the point of initial contact, and it was not limited to those applicants who required emergency assistance.

It was not followed as a departmental policy but as an administrative expedient to free staff time for the performance of another task, namely, redetermination of eligibility.

APPENDIX K
FORM USED BY THE CUYAHOGA COUNTY WELFARE DEPARTMENT FOR GENERAL RELIEF AND ALL EMERGENCIES

APPLICATION FOR ASSISTANCE
(AFFIDAVIT)

SURNAME _____ FIRST NAME _____ CASE NO. _____ Yes | No

ADDRESS _____ TELEPHONE _____ IS TELEPHONE IN YOUR NAME _____

PERSONS IN NEED

THE PERSON OR PERSONS LISTED BELOW ARE IN NEED AND MY FINANCIAL RESOURCES ARE NOT ADEQUATE TO MAINTAIN THEM.

	BIRTH DATE		BIRTH DATE		BIRTH DATE
1.		4.		7.	
2.		5.		8.	
3.		6.		9.	

AID TO BLIND ONLY
1. YEAR BLINDNESS OCCURRED _____ 2. WERE YOU THEN A RESIDENT OF OHIO _____

AID TO DEPENDENT CHILDREN ONLY
1. THE CHILDREN NAMED ARE DEPRIVED OF PARENTAL SUPPORT BECAUSE OF _____
2. NAME CHILDREN 16 TO 18 ATTENDING SCHOOL _____

RESIDENCE—Give Residence Past Nine Years

STATE	DATE (MO. and YR.) FROM TO	COUNTY	DATE (MO. and YR.) FROM TO	CITY	DATE (MO. and YR.) FROM TO

EMPLOYMENT (Include Each Person in Household 16 Years of Age and Over)

NAME	NAME OF FIRM OR EMPLOYER	ADDRESS	EMPLOYED FROM TO	POSITION	WAGE

HAVE YOU REGISTERED WITH O.S.E.S.? _____ DATE _____ NO. _____
HAVE YOU FILED FOR UNEMPLOYMENT COMPENSATION _____
HAVE YOU FILED FOR INDUSTRIAL COMPENSATION _____
HAVE YOU FILED FOR OLD AGE & SURVIVORS INSURANCE _____
DO YOU GIVE PERMISSION FOR RELEASE OF INFORMATION FROM O.S.E.S.? _____

BENEFITS

ARE YOU RECEIVING
- VETERAN'S BENEFITS? _____ AMOUNT $ _____
- SICK BENEFITS? _____ AMOUNT $ _____
- OTHER? _____ AMOUNT $ _____

HAVE YOU RECEIVED ANY
- INHERITANCES? _____ AMOUNT $ _____
- PERSONAL INJURY SETTLEMENT FOR YOURSELF OR CHILDREN? _____ AMOUNT $ _____
- GIFTS _____ AMOUNT $ _____
- OTHER ASSETS? _____ AMOUNT $ _____

SPECIFY WHICH, AND CIRCUMSTANCES _____

BANK ACCOUNTS AND INVESTMENTS

DO YOU OR ANY MEMBER OF YOUR HOUSEHOLD HAVE ANY ACCOUNTS IN BANKS (CLOSED OR OPEN), OR ANY STOCKS, BONDS, POSTAL SAVINGS OR OTHER INVESTMENTS? _____

NAME, ADDRESS AND ACCOUNT NO. OF BANK OR COMPANY

_____ AMOUNT $ _____
_____ AMOUNT $ _____
_____ AMOUNT $ _____
_____ AMOUNT $ _____

CWI-1546.3   REV. 4/1/66

OTHER RESOURCES

DO YOU OR ANY MEMBERS OF YOUR HOUSEHOLD HAVE ANY RENTAL OR OTHER INCOME AT THIS TIME?_____
IF SO, STATE SOURCE, AMOUNT, AND PERSON RECEIVING SAME. (EMPLOYMENT, UNEMPLOYMENT, COMPENSATION BENEFITS, ROOMERS, PENSIONS, VETERANS COMPENSATIONS, INDUSTRIAL COMPENSATION, ALIMONY, SICK BENEFITS, ASSISTANCE FROM FRIENDS, RELATIVES, CHURCHES, ALIMONY OR SUPPORT PAYMENTS?

PERSON RECEIVING	SOURCE	AMT.	PERSON RECEIVING	SOURCE	AMT.

HAVE ANY OF THE CHILDREN LEFT HOME TO LIVE WITH SOMEONE ELSE?_____ NAMES_____
_____ WITH WHOM?_____
HAVE ANY OF YOU CHILDREN JOINED THE ARMED FORCES?_____
IF SO, DO YOU RECEIVE AN ALLOWANCE OR ALLOTMENT?_____ AMOUNT_____

REAL ESTATE

DO YOU OR ANY MEMBER OF YOUR FAMILY OWN REAL ESTATE?_____
WHERE?_____
DATE OF PURCHASE_____ PURCHASE PRICE_____
PRESENT TAX VALUATION_____ (USE PROPERTY FORM)
HAVE YOU OR ANY MEMBER OF YOUR FAMILY TRANSFERRED OR ASSIGNED PROPERTY WITHIN THE LAST TWO YEARS?_____

INSURANCE

DO YOU OR ANY MEMBERS OF YOUR HOUSEHOLD CARRY LIFE INSURANCE?_____
HOW MANY POLICIES?_____ (USE INSURANCE FORM)

AUTOMOBILES — TRUCKS OR T.V. OWNED BY MEMBERS OF HOUSEHOLD

DO YOU OWN A CAR	YEAR	LICENSE NUMBER	IN WHOSE NAME PURCHASED	DATE PURCHASED	AMOUNT OWED	TO WHOM
DO YOU OWN A T.V.						

DEBTS (Including Loans and Real Estate Mortgages)

NAME OF CREDITOR	ADDRESS	ITEM FURNISHED	ORIGINAL AMOUNT	BALANCE OWED	LAST DATE	PAYMENT AMOUNT

DO YOU UNDERSTAND THAT YOU MUST ADVISE YOUR CASEWORKER IMMEDIATELY IF YOU SECURE EMPLOYMENT, MOVE, RECEIVE ANY ASSETS OR IF THERE IS A CHANGE IN YOUR FAMILY STATUS?

—"NO PERSON SHALL BE ELIGIBLE FOR POOR RELIEF IF HE HAS TRANSFERRED PROPERTY DURING THE TWO YEARS PRECEDING HIS APPLICATION FOR THE PURPOSE OF SECURING POOR RELIEF. NO PERSON SHALL FRAUDULENTLY MISREPRESENT OR FRAUDULENTLY CONCEAL FACTS WHICH AFFECT HIS NEED FOR POOR RELIEF." Rev. G.C. 5113.13

"WHOEVER VIOLATES SECTION 5113.13 OF THE REVISED CODE SHALL BE FINED NOT MORE THAN ONE THOUSAND DOLLARS OR IMPRISONED NOT LESS THAN ONE OR MORE THAN THREE YEARS; IF THE "TOTAL AMOUNT OF THE RELIEF SO FALSELY OBTAINED IS LESS THAN ONE HUNDRED DOLLARS, SUCH PERSON SHALL BE FINED NOT MORE THAN FIVE HUNDRED DOLLARS OR IMPRISONED NOT MORE THAN THREE MONTHS OR BOTH." Rev. G.C. 5113.99

AFFIDAVIT

IF BY MARK: HIS OR HER

1. WITNESS   NAME & ADDRESS
_____   _____
                                                                          SIGNATURE OR MARK OF APPLICANT
2._____
SWORN TO AND SUBSCRIBED BEFORE ME
THIS_____DAY OF_____
_____ 19____   _____
                                                                          INTERVIEWER

APPENDIX L
TABLE OF ORGANIZATION, CUYAHOGA COUNTY WELFARE DEPARTMENT

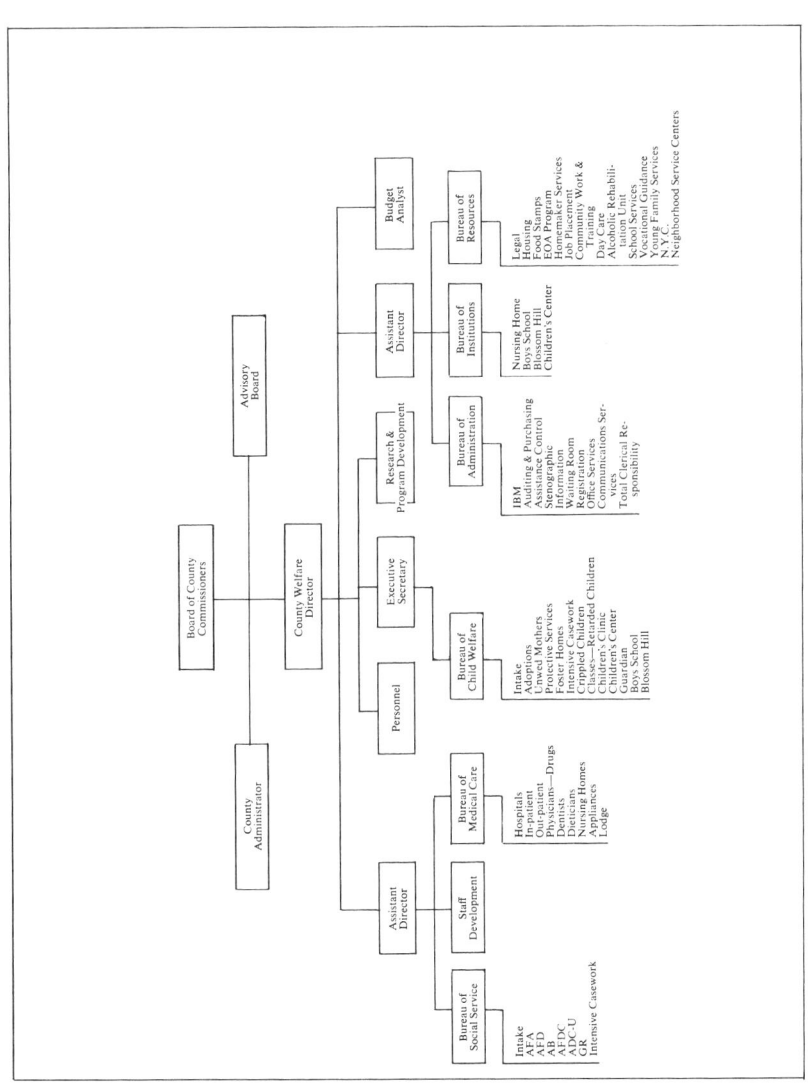

APPENDIX M
APPLICATION FOR FAIR HEARING, PRESCRIBED BY OHIO STATE DEPARTMENT OF PUBLIC WELFARE, DIVISION OF SOCIAL ADMINISTRATION

PRESCRIBED BY STATE DEPARTMENT OF PUBLIC WELFARE, DIVISION OF SOCIAL ADMINISTRATION

APPLICATION FOR HEARING

.... 19 ....

Re: ....

Application No. ....

TO DEPARTMENT OF PUBLIC WELFARE
DIVISION OF SOCIAL ADMINISTRATION
OAK STREET AT NINTH
COLUMBUS, OHIO

GENTLEMEN:

I have requested assistance from the .... County
aid to blind .... administration.
aid to dependent children ....
aid to the permanently and totally disabled ....

The county administration has taken the following action on my request:

Check here

.... 1. Refused to accept my application.
.... 2. Rejected my application for assistance
.... 3. Failed to make a decision on my application
.... 4. Awarded me an inadequate grant
.... 5. Reduced my grant
.... 6. Terminated my grant
.... 7. ....other (specify)

I am dissatisfied with the action taken and request a hearing of my case as provided by law.

Sincerely yours,

Witness if signed by mark:

....
                                                                  (Name of applicant)

....
                                                                  (Address of applicant)

Mail both copies of this application to department of public welfare

DSA 161
CW-1946

APPENDIX N
COMPARISON OF AGE AND EMPLOYMENT STATUS OF CUYAHOGA COUNTY RECIPIENTS AND NATIONAL RECIPIENTS, 1967

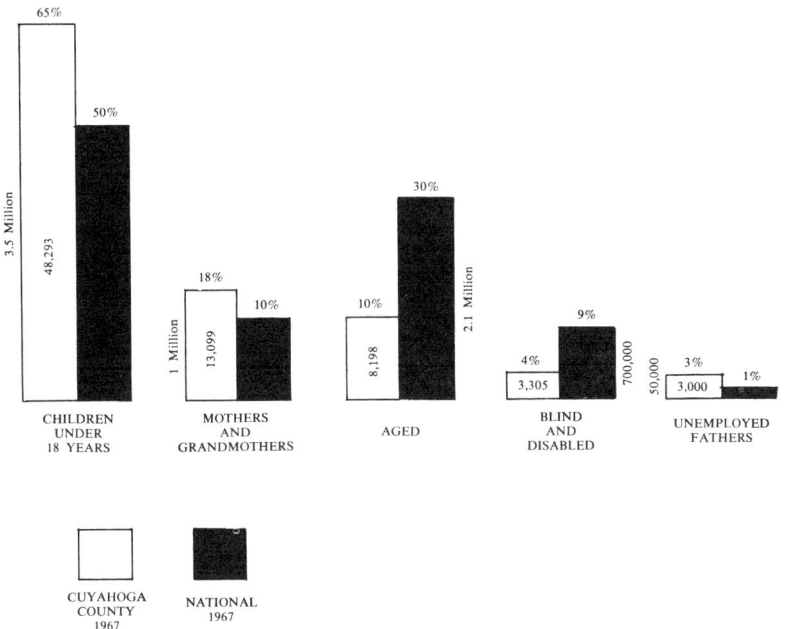

APPENDIX O
EMPLOYMENT AND TRAINING

JOB TRAINING, EMPLOYMENT STANDARDS, AND ENTRY-PAY LEVELS

If the elimination of dependency and a reduction in depressed areas' unemployment rate are goals of the work training programs, consideration must be given to incentives provided for applicants and enrollees. Job entry-pay levels, and the training work experience provided often offers little inducement for the hard-core unemployed to seek training and jobs.

The Title V program in 1967 placed some enrollees in jobs paying $220 per month ($2,640 per year). AIM/JOBS, after four months of operation, indicated that 15% of the enrollees were placed on jobs paying less than $1.70 per hour.[1] The poverty level for a family of four was established at $3,200 in November, 1967, indicating we are investing large sums in preparing people for poverty wage jobs. The Cuyahoga County Welfare Department has to keep many of the clients trained under Title V and placed in employment on supplemental relief.

The 22 Special Manpower Programs reported that of the 2,500 job placements during the first six months of 1967, the majority were placed in service and unskilled occupations.[2] Although the Mayor's Commission does not have data on the average wages paid on these jobs, the type of service jobs on which many enrollees are placed pay below the minimum wage. In some instances enrollees can net more income in training stipends than on some jobs. This reduces incentive. "Work experience" and "work training" programs for groundskeepers for the City Departments of Recreation, Cemeteries,

---

[1] AIM/JOBS Report, October 27, 1967.
[2] Manpower Planning and Development Commission, Welfare Federation of Cleveland, September, 1967.

and Shade Trees and for workers on city refuse trucks offer almost no real training.

Another major problem stems from often unrealistic job standards established by some employers. Many training program enrollees, considered job-ready, are frozen out of employment due to examinations which may or may not relate to job ability. AIM/JOBS has attempted to have employers use the assessment evaluation developed by the training program. The Ohio State Employment Service has been able to convince some employers of the need to evaluate and lower entry-level standards. Service personnel see this as a major need.[3] Administrators of the training programs support this position.

RACIAL DISCRIMINATION IN EMPLOYMENT AND IN CRAFT UNIONS

Traditional restrictions on opportunities for Negro citizens are reflected in a special labor report of the U.S. Department of Labor in 1966.[4] The Negro labor force was found to be concentrated in the less secure, less desirable, and less rewarding jobs. Nearly one-third of all employed urban Negroes were in service occupations and one in ten held jobs in private households; 56% of employed Negro women held service jobs, of which half were in private households. The largest proportion of Negro men worked as operatives or laborers—jobs diminishing in significance with changes in technology and economy.

Racial discrimination in the job market is still a way of life in the nation. The craft unions in the building trades have traditionally practiced racial exclusion of Negroes. Though the construction industry is among the largest in the nation, it is plagued with an acute shortage of skilled labor.

The establishment of equal job opportunities for all citizens would provide additional jobs for the unemployed and subemployed at pay levels that would provide both financial security and motivation to persons who are trainees, relief recip-

---

[3] Mr. Mitchell Stanton, Ohio State Employment Service, April 1, 1968.
[4] *Poverty Areas of our Major Cities*, Special Labor Force Report No. 75, U.S. Department of Labor, 1966.

ients, or potential recipients. Many persons who are working and receiving relief supplementation could be placed in employment which would provide for complete severance from relief rolls.

COMMUNITY SERVICE EMPLOYMENT PROJECTS FOR THE UNEMPLOYED

The unemployment rate in metropolitan Cleveland is approximately 2.4%, one of the lowest in the country. While there is no precise data on the depressed area unemployed, a gross estimate can be determined. The U.S. Department of Labor reports that the unemployment rate in Cleveland's inner city was 15.6% in 1967.[5] In terms of numbers, the Bureau of Census 1965 report showed approximately 12,800 unemployed. Additionally, there was a nonparticipation rate of 14.7% (8,000) among men between the ages of 20 and 64. The difference between the number of males to number of females showed that there were 10,000 males who had "disappeared" and were not counted. There are currently 13,000 adult females, recipients of AFDC, who are not counted in the labor force but, all things being equal, might be employed.[6] The 1966 *Unemployed Out-of-School Youth Survey*, conducted by the Cleveland Board of Education, indicated there were possibly 5,000 unemployed youth in the depressed areas.

Taking all these factors into consideration, the number of unemployed in the depressed areas might be grossly estimated to be 49,000 persons. This estimate does not consider the "employability" of this population.

In the first six months of 1967 the 22 Special Manpower Programs in Cleveland placed 2,500 persons in jobs. This is only 30% of the original 8,000 enrollees. (Placement, in many instances, means referral to a job.) Follow-up after placement was reported as providing for less than half of those placed, or about 1,200.[7]

AIM/JOBS placed 770 formerly jobless participants through

---

[5]*A Sharper Look at Unemployment in U.S. Cities and Slums*, U.S. Department of Labor, 1967.

[6]*Characteristics of Selected Neighborhoods in Cleveland*.

[7]Manpower Planning and Development Commission of the Welfare Federation of Cleveland, September, 1967.

December, 1967, which was approximately 40% of their 1,976 enrollees. Since figures were not available on the 22 Special Manpower Programs, if we estimate that they continued placement at the rate established during the first six months (2,500), we can assume that roughly 5,770 enrollees were employed in 1967. This figure represents 12% of the estimated unemployed in the depressed areas.

DEVELOPMENT OF INDUSTRY IN DEPRESSED AREAS

The Standard Oil Company is perhaps the largest of the many employers who have recently left the City of Cleveland. Coupled with this loss is the rapid migration of industry to the suburbs. The loss of industry leaves the unskilled behind without employment and compounds the unemployment problem. Since it is recognized that the bulk of the depressed areas' unemployed are unskilled or semiskilled persons, it would be desirable for industry to meet their needs for employment, and in proximity to their places of residence.

Cleveland, with its waterways and complex railroad system, has much to offer in the way of benefits to large industry. It also has thousands of acres of land that have been taken off the tax duplicate through urban renewal, and are yet undeveloped.

The State Legislature has reduced the growth rate of the personal property tax by reducing the assessments on inventories by 7% in 1968. No relief from this static state of the income from taxes is foreseen until 1970 when the current real estate development in downtown Cleveland becomes a part of the tax duplicate.

Precedent has been established in the Watts area of Los Angeles relative to developing industry and providing jobs for residents in depressed areas. Major incentive and pride in employment were developed by providing management positions for nonwhite personnel. The development of industry in areas of high unemployment within the City of Cleveland would provide jobs easily accessible to persons who have difficulty seeking employment in outlying areas. The same motivational incentives inherent in the Watts program could be developed locally. Inner-city industries would provide employment for many AFDC mothers who find it difficult to accept employment in outlying areas. Industry geared to the skill or low-skill level of residents would open new job opportunities for the hard-core unemployed.

TRANSPORTATION

The movement of business and industry away from the central city has created major obstacles to employment of inner-city residents, barriers much greater than most people perceive. Without automobiles or money for public transportation, and living mostly within the confines of slum neighborhoods, many have little, if any, knowledge of the new plants which are springing up on the outskirts of the city.

Currently, one of the major breweries in Cleveland provides a bus to transport office employees from the plant to major transit centers. Revamping of current bus schedules would not solve the transit problem. Roads are constructed by public subsidy to effect automobile transportation and provide ease of access to industrial sites. However, persons who use public transportation enjoy no such subsidy or special assistance.

Plans to increase the employability of inner-city residents by stepping up job training for the unemployed and subemployed must be supported by the provision of job opportunities. The existence of major obstacles in reaching places of employment will have a limiting affect on the number of persons who will seek employment in suburban areas.

EMPLOYMENT OF WOMEN

The job-finding difficulties of workers in poverty areas are often compounded by discrimination on the basis of race, ethnic background, age, and sex. In the case of young women with salable skills, there is the added factor of the employer reluctance to hire workers who may soon leave their jobs because of early marriage or childbearing.

In Cleveland's 22 Special Manpower Programs men outnumbered women about 4,600 to 3,400 in the first six months of 1967. AIM/JOBS applicants are about 75% male. Administrators of two Special Manpower Programs specifically mentioned the need for more employment opportunities for women, especially for female heads of households. Due to special problems in the placement of women and stress on male employment, the recruitment of women has low priority in some programs.

AIM/JOBS indicates that women over 35 years, teenage girls (17–18 years), and nonskilled women are difficult to employ and that most jobs available pay poorly. Women on public assistance often net less by working than if they remain unemployed. Ohio State Employment Service, on the other hand, relates the great need for women with office skills, high entry-pay levels, and the promise of continued employment.

EMPLOYMENT OF AFDC MOTHERS

The training and employment program proposed under the 1967 Amendments to the Social Security Act is directed primarily to AFDC mothers; currently in Cleveland there are 13,000 on the rolls. Mandatory referrals to job training and employment could present major problems related to the kind of employment which mothers might be forced to take. All programs have problems placing women in meaningful jobs.

Currently, the Ohio State Employment Service has more than 2,000 unfilled jobs, but many are in low-paying service occupations. There is a chance that these might be used as a dumping ground for AFDC mothers under the provisions of the 1967 Amendments. In addition, there is no consideration in the legislation regarding working conditions, minimum wages, hardships related to reaching employment, hours, supportive counseling, or restraints to prevent caseworkers from using the threat of undesirable employment to force compliance from clients in other areas.

If the Amendments are to carry out the intent of the Social Security Act and provide for employment under humane conditions, specific regulations should be developed to protect AFDC mothers from exploitation. There should be rules and regulations covering the selection process for training and employment to prevent indiscriminate assignment of mothers to training and job situations.

DAY CARE FACILITIES FOR WORKING MOTHERS

The lack of day care facilities is a major deterrent to gainful employment to mothers receiving welfare. Of 5,292,000 persons in the labor market in September, 1966, the U.S. Department of Labor found 435,000 nonparticipants who cited child care arrangements as the reason for unemployment. Locally, the administrators and staff of the County Welfare Department indicate that many AFDC mothers would prefer employment to public assistance but are hindered by child care problems. A recent study in New York City revealed that 70% of the AFDC mothers preferred employment to public assistance.

Industry recently has largely ignored the possibility of developing child care facilities for the working mother. However, during the acute labor shortage of the World War II period, industry and government cooperated in providing such facilities to attract women into employment situations. Many European industries provide child care facilities for working mothers. Tentative beginnings have been made recently in the United States.

Employment and training of AFDC mothers requires facilities for children at the site of employment. The convenience of site facilities and the provision for some shared time between mothers and children could be an inducement for many AFDC mothers to seek employment in industries which provide decent wages.

According to a national survey conducted by the Children's Bureau of the U.S. Welfare Administration, one out of every five working mothers from families with an income of less than $3,000 was attempting to combine child care with work at the job. In many communities it is not unusual for working mothers to keep older children home on alternate days to care for younger siblings.

Under the provisions of the Social Security Amendments of 1967, the federal government will provide up to 85% of the cost of special day care centers in 1968 and 75% thereafter if they are approved by the state as meeting state standards for licensing. A local public subsidy should be considered where necessary.

Provisions for day care for personnel in some hospitals are currently underway. Experience indicates that this service does not work well without the supervision of professional staff. The varying levels of adequacy in services points up the need for a state code with licensing provisions. The City of Cleveland code was developed more than 40 years ago and does not reflect the most current standards for child day care.

SERVICE INDUSTRY EMPLOYMENT PROGRAM

While the placement of low-income and underemployed individuals in jobs with large firms offers the best opportunity for such persons to rise out of poverty, it is not the only solution to the problem. If the objective is to reduce dependency as rapidly as possible, attention must also be paid to developing jobs, often in the service industry, with small employers, including homeowners.

In light of the low wages and fringe benefits of domestics and service employees, an advocate such as a union or the City of Cleveland is needed to guarantee a minimum wage, no lower than the federal minimum, applicable to all such jobs performed by adults.

A program to develop attractive, stable jobs for domestic and service workers would need an intermediary between employers who want assistance—and are willing to provide decent wages and standards—and people who want to work. Such an intermediary would function best if it modeled itself after the private Manpower Inc. or Kelly Girl organizations. The employers and the employees served would both require considerable counseling. This service, under government auspices, should not be performed at a profit but with a public subsidy.

Some private employment agencies might be interested in developing unique employment services, to assist in placing the unemployed in service jobs, if a subsidy was provided for needed counseling services. This service could be either on a profit or nonprofit basis with contractual agreements with the city related to procedures and modes of operation.

Many persons are seeking part-time employment and could benefit from a program of job-sharing. In some situations, two persons seeking part-time employment could share a full-time job by each working 20 hours a week.

YOUTH EMPLOYMENT

Children who are recipients of AFDC and youth of low-income families have major difficulty in obtaining adequate and sufficient clothing to attend school or funds to purchase supplies and pay for other necessities. Many children become discouraged and disinterested in school due to special problems related to indigency. It is estimated that over 4,000 children drop out of school annually, the majority for economic reasons. They become dropouts without work skills and many do not have a parent model to establish expected norms in employment situations. The Cleveland Board of Education reported recently that through the In-School Neighborhood Youth Corps Program they have seen a decline in dropouts due to additional monies supplementing family incomes and providing for the youth's expenses. These problems were considered in the 1967 Social Security legislation that provides for employment of school age youth on public assistance without reduction in the family budget.

FOLLOW-UP AND SUPPORTIVE SERVICES FOR SPECIAL MANPOWER PROGRAMS

Administrators of the Special Manpower Programs in Cleveland require better follow-up services and increased staff support to stabilize trainee work goals and provide the necessary supportive services to keep the trainee employed. In addition to this pressing need, there is also a high loss of potential enrollees in referral between programs.

Of the 10 Special Manpower Programs which have job placement services, only one had no follow-up after placement. However, among those who did follow-up, practices varied greatly. Some maintained contact with the client and his employer only so long as the client remained under the auspices of the Special Manpower Program. With others, a staff person would check with the client and employer 30 to 60 days after placement.[8]

The four Special Manpower Programs which provided in-

---

[8]Manpower Planning and Development Commission of the Welfare Federation of Cleveland, September, 1967.

formation about job retention estimated that about 5% of those placed retained their jobs one month or less. Another 25% were estimated to have kept their jobs from one to three months, about 18% from three to six months, and about 52% for six months or more. The job retention problem reveals that supportive services are an absolute necessity.[9]

With 8,000 applicants in the Special Manpower Programs during the first six months of 1967, and 2,500 jobs secured for these applicants, follow-up on those not placed in employment is a necessity. In addition, among the eight programs which provided information on the number of persons who failed to complete the recommended program during the first six months of 1967, the percentage varied from 10% to 36%. Two programs reported dropout rates of more than 30%, one 20%, and five 10% to 15%. For these clients, there is also a need for staff follow-up.[10]

Reports from two training program directors suggested the need for extension of time allotted for remedial programs and job orientation. Many enrollees are forced to terminate due to time limitations for job orientation and job readiness programs. If extensions were granted, many would be helped to move into training and employment situations.

---

[9]*Ibid.*
[10]*Ibid.*

APPENDIX P
SOCIAL SECURITY AMENDMENTS OF 1967

The original intent of the public assistance programs, within Social Security legislation, was to provide financial assistance and social services to strengthen and maintain family life in time of need. In the 1967 amendments there are a number of features which provide for increased services and liberalizing of previous welfare practices. There are, however, several elements in the new legislation which are coercive and restrictive as they apply to the poor. These amendments apparently reflect not only a punitive mood within Congress towards welfare clientele, but probably reflect as well a negative view from the public as a whole to the poor on welfare, based largely on misinformation as to the nature of the problem.

The amendments cover services in several publicly assisted programs; however major emphasis is directed toward changing the AFDC program. In the new legislation, there is a reversal of the philosophy inherent in the original legislation which provided financial assistance for the purpose of keeping the mother with dependent children in the home. The law now puts emphasis on work training and employment of the mother to the point where the mother may have to leave the home, whether she considers this proper or improper for care of her children. Provision is made for service supports considered necessary to help the AFDC mother become employable. The new law also restricts the number of recipients who will be supported by federal funds. The expanded use of vendor payments marks a further retreat from the principle of cash benefits, which give recipient parents the right and responsibility of making decisions regarding the care of their children. Family and child service features are provided in an endeavor to strengthen family life and move families toward social and financial independence. The concerns of the Mayor's Commission regarding some of the major provisions of the bill relate

WORK INCENTIVE PROGRAM

Under this legislation a "work incentive program" will provide for training for AFDC mothers and will be administered by the U.S. Department of Labor. The public welfare agencies will be required to refer all "appropriate" AFDC clients to the state employment agency. Those excluded include the ill and incapacitated, children in school or under the age of 16, persons whose presence is needed in the home because of the incapacity of illness of another member of the household, persons who are distant from training programs, and those who are too old to be considered for training and employment.

Under this law any person who refuses to participate in the program and who has been considered "appropriate" for training and/or employment will be removed from the relief rolls. Assistance will be provided for the dependents (children) through protective and vendor payments. Families whose earnings are below the minimum budget standards will continue receiving supplementary assistance plus 20% of the wage. The first $30 earned and one-third of the remaining income from jobs will be retained by families. Special work projects will be developed for persons who are not able to benefit from training or cannot hold regular jobs due to educational or other deficiencies. Workers will be paid at or above the national minimum wage if it applies to the particular job on which they are placed.

The work provisions are directed towards providing security for families and reducing the relief rolls. However, there are hazards related to those programs. One hazard lies in the exercise of judgment of welfare workers or administrators in determining who is an "appropriate" mother for employment. Protection for workers against abuse of this judgment is needed. Moreover, the AFDC mother will no longer have the choice other mothers have as to whether she works or provides care for her family. Testimony from caseworkers and clients reveals that the majority of the AFDC mothers would prefer employment. However, many feel a responsibility to care for their young children. To be able to exclude mothers from the assistance program in the event employment is refused is punitive and coercive. This further demeans the AFDC mother and subjects her to the value judgments of welfare agency personnel.

FEDERAL FREEZE ON AFDC FUNDS

Federal financial participation in AFDC programs will be held at a given level after July 1, 1968. The federal matching funds will be determined by the number of AFDC children in the state who were receiving aid as of January 1, 1968. This means that the state can either pay the total cost for AFDC recipients who enter the program after January 1, 1968, or reduce its current levels of payment to stay within the state budget allocations for welfare. This proviso in effect discriminates against persons in need, who otherwise meet the same conditions of eligibility as persons on the AFDC rolls prior to the cutoff date. The historic recalcitrance of many state administrations and legislatures to meet the welfare needs of citizens suggests that recipients will be hurt by the freeze regulations. New families on the rolls could be forced to accept General Relief and lose the few benefits that accrue to the AFDC recipients. Eligibility requirements could be changed by states in an effort to further limit the number of AFDC recipients.

UNEMPLOYED FATHERS AND AID TO DEPENDENT CHILDREN

The current law gives to the states the option to include unemployed fathers under the AFDC program if they do not have such provisions. It further stipulates that, to be eligible, the father must have had six or more quarters of employment in any 13-month quarter within one year of application for assistance. The providing of this option to states encourages a continuation of the current practice of variation in eligibility requirements and service and assistance levels among several states. The stipulations related to eligibility of fathers makes it more difficult for men to become eligible and reduces the number of families with male heads of households that will be covered by the AFDC program. This can serve to encourage the economically insecure father to desert his family.

PROTECTIVE PAYMENTS

One of the major advances in the Social Security Act of 1935 was the principle of cash benefits in public assistance, as opposed to the demeaning "relief-in-kind" or use of vouchers. The principle of cash benefits recognized the basic importance of freedom to make decisions as a means of maintaining and strengthening parents' dignity, authority in the home, and self-dependence. There is overwhelming evidence that any risk that parents will use benefits unwisely is far outweighed by the demoralization and dependency inherent in relief-in-kind. Where necessary, it is possible to appoint a guardian to handle a client's affairs.

The 1967 Social Security Amendments have greatly accelerated a previous trend away from the principle of cash payments. In 1962, Congress made it possible for states to place 5% of their AFDC families under so-called Protective Payments, noncash relief or voucher payments. But only those states providing 100% of need could use this device; Ohio, for instance, was excluded because it provided less than 100%. The 1967 Amendments now allow states to place 10% of their AFDC families under Protective Payments, and all states may participate, whether or not they are paying 100% of need. In addition, states can make unlimited use of Protective Payments to the families of persons who refuse to accept work or training assignments.

We are concerned that welfare departments may use the broadened Protective Payments provision, not to "protect" anybody, but to control clients' lives and to punish them.

DAY CARE CENTERS FOR CHILDREN

Among the supportive services provided under the new amendments is the program for day care centers for AFDC mothers. These centers will be utilized for children when mothers are involved in training programs or in employment situations. This program will be welcomed by many mothers who have child care responsibilities and who would prefer employment to public assistance. Day care may not, however, be the most appropriate plan for some mothers.

The previous comments relate to only those provisions in

the 1967 Amendments which give cause for concern. There are a number of features in this legislation which reflect some progress in trying to meet human needs. Our interest is to increase the effectiveness of those provisions by eliminating or changing features which can be punitive and coercive in their effects.

APPENDIX Q
MISCELLANEOUS TABLES

Table Q.1a. Comparison of Public and Voluntary Funds for Social Insurances, Veterans Programs and Welfare, and Health, Recreation and Other Services in Cleveland, by Field of Service and Source of Funds, 1965 (In thousands of dollars)

PROGRAM AND FIELD OF SERVICE[a]	TOTAL FUNDS		PUBLIC FUNDS		CONTRIBUTIONS					FEES		OTHER INCOME[c]	
					UNITED APPEAL		OTHER[b]					
Total (all programs)	542,731	100%	383,104	70.6%	11,462	2.1%	6,066	1.1%	126,468	23.3%	15,631	2.9%
Social insurances[d]	226,485	100	226,485	100	—	—	—	—	—	—	—	—
Veterans programs[d]	54,370	100	54,370	100	—	—	—	—	—	—	—	—
Welfare, health, recreation, and other services (total)	261,876	100	102,249	39.0	11,462	4.4	6,066	2.3	126,468	48.3	15,631	6.0
Welfare services (total)	71,941	100	56,863	79.0	4,175	5.8	1,266	1.8	4,788	6.7	4,849	6.7
Public assistance service	40,551	100	40,551	100	—	—	—	—	—	—	—	—
Other economic assistance and social adjustment services	31,390	100	16,312	52.0	4,175	13.3	1,266	4.0	4,788	15.3	4,849	15.4
Health services (total)	166,568	100	35,227	21.1	2,465	1.5	3,801	2.3	116,169	69.7	8,906	5.4
Hospitals, clinics and nursing homes other than mental	143,036	100	20,532	14.4	1,188	.8	1,780	1.2	111,947	78.3	7,589	5.3
Mental hospitals, clinics, and nursing homes	15,887	100	11,221	70.6	367	2.3	247	1.6	3,600	22.7	452	2.8
Other health services	7,645	100	3,474	45.5	910	11.9	1,774	23.2	622	8.1	865	11.3
Recreation services	14,262	100	3,957	27.8	2,923	20.5	616	4.3	5,495	38.5	1,271	8.9
Central services	3,498	100	595	17.0	1,899	54.3	383	10.9	16	.5	605	17.3
Public aid, emergency aid, and surplus food[d]	3,040	100	3,040	100	—	—	—	—	—	—	—	—
Work training programs[d]	2,567	100	2,567	100	—	—	—	—	—	—	—	—

[a]See table Q.1b for specific services in each category. [b]Includes sectarian funds and gifts. [c]Includes endowments, investments, and other earnings. [d]Estimate of expenditures.

SOURCE: "1965 Study of Expenditures for Health, Welfare & Recreation Service in Cuyahoga County," Research Department, Welfare Federation of Cleveland, 1966.

Table Q.1b. Services Included Under Social Insurances, Veterans Programs and Welfare, and Health, Welfare, Recreation, and Other Services

SOCIAL INSURANCE

O.A.S.D.H.I. (Old Age Survivors Disability and Health Insurance)
Railroad Retirement
Railroad Unemployment Insurance
Railroad Temporary Disability Insurance
State Unemployment Insurance
Workmens' Compensation

VETERANS PROGRAMS

Pensions and Compensation
Health and Medical Services

HEALTH, WELFARE, RECREATION, AND OTHER SERVICES

Public Assistance Services
  General Assistance
  Categorical Assistance Programs
    Aid to Families with Dependent Children
    Old Age Assistance
    Aid to the Blind
    Aid to the Permanently and Totally Disabled
Other Economic Assistance and Social Adjustment Services
  Institutions for Adults
    Shelters for Transients and Homeless
    Institutions for Domiciliary Care of Adults
  Institutions for Children
    Institutions for Dependent Children
    Institutions for Delinquent Children
  Family and Child Care Services, Noninstitutional
    Family Service, Protective and Foster Home Care, Court-Related Social Services for Adults, Special Services for Children with Behavior Problems
  Other
    Day Nurseries and Preschool Programs
    Head Start Programs
    Programs for Mentally Retarded Children
    Maternity Home Care
    Employment Training and Placement for the Economically Disadvantaged
    Specialized Nonmedical Services for the Handicapped
    Other
Hospitals, Clinics, and Nursing Homes (other than Mental)
  General and Allied Special (except Rehabilitation Programs)
  Rehabilitation Programs
  Chronic
  Tuberculosis
Mental Hospitals, Clinics, and Nursing Homes
  Institutions for the Mentally Disturbed

Institutions for Mental Defectives or Epileptics
Out-Patient Psychiatric Clinics
Residential Treatment Centers

Other Health Services
Public Health Nursing and Social Services
  Public Health Nursing Services
  School Nursing Services
  School Medical and Dental Services
Community Health Services
Other Health Services

Recreation Services
Public Recreation Services
Voluntary Building-Centered Programs
  YMCA and YWCA
  Jewish Community Centers, YMHA, and YWHA
  Settlements, Neighborhood Houses, and Community Centers (other than Jewish)
  Boys Clubs and Girls Clubs
Scouting and Camp Fire
Other Voluntary Recreation Services

Central Services
Federal Financing and Community Planning
  Federated Financing
  Community Health and Welfare Planning
  Other Council-type Central Services
Other Central Services

Public Aid, Emergency Aid, and Surplus Food to Needy Families
Work Training Programs
M.D.T.A. (Manpower Development Training Act)
Job Corps
Project for 50's
Project Peace
Urban League O.J.T. (On-the-Job Training)
Work Study Program

Table Q.2. Percentage Distribution of Funds for Welfare, Health, and Recreation Services, by Field of Service and Source of Funds in Cleveland, 1965 (In thousands of dollars)

FIELD OF SERVICE	TOTAL FUNDS		PUBLIC FUNDS		UNITED APPEAL AND OTHER CONTRIB.		FEES		OTHER INCOME	
Total	261,876	100%	102,249	100%	17,528	100%	126,468	100%	15,631	100%
Welfare services (total)	71,941	27.5	56,863	55.7	5,441	31.0	4,788	3.8	4,849	31.0
Public assistance service	40,551	15.5	40,551	39.7	—	—	—	—	—	—
Other economic assistance and social adjustment services	31,390	12.0	16,312	16.0	5,441	31.0	4,788	3.8	4,849	31.0
Health services (total)	166,568	63.6	35,227	34.4	6,266	35.7	116,169	91.8	8,906	57.0
Hospitals, clinics, and nursing homes (other than mental)	143,036	54.6	20,532	20.1	2,968	16.9	111,947	88.5	7,589	48.6
Mental hospitals, clinics, and nursing homes	15,887	6.1	11,221	11.0	614	3.5	3,600	2.8	452	2.9
Other health services	7,645	2.9	3,474	3.3	2,684	15.3	622	.5	865	5.5
Recreation services	14,262	5.4	3,957	3.8	3,539	20.3	5,495	4.4	1,271	8.1
Central services	3,498	1.3	595	.6	2,282	13.0	16	.01	605	3.9
Public aid, emergency aid, and surplus food	3,040	1.2	3,040	3.0	—	—	—	—	—	—
Work training programs	2,567	1.0	2,567	2.5	—	—	—	—	—	—

Table Q.3. Estimates of Population of Cuyahoga County, 1965, by Poverty and Nonpoverty Areas

	POPULATION	PER CENT OF TOTAL
Poverty areas, Cleveland	331,898	19
Nonpoverty areas, Cleveland	516,210	29
Suburbs	910,893	52
Total	1,759,001	100

SOURCES: Ohio State Health Department; U.S. Special Census for Cleveland, 1965, Series P. 23, No. 21.

Table Q.4. Distribution of Funds by Voluntary and Public Welfare Agencies, Cuyahoga County, 1966[a]

AGENCY AND GEOGRAPHIC AREA	TOTAL EXPENDITURES	PER CENT OF TOTAL	PER CAPITA EXPENDITURES FOR TOTAL POPULATION
Voluntary—Red Feather and other			
Poverty areas, Cleveland	$ 5,148,188	25	$ 15.51
Nonpoverty areas, Cleveland	4,887,248	24	9.47
Suburbs	10,299,406	51	11.31
Total	20,334,842	100	11.56
Public			
Poverty areas, Cleveland	$50,134,584	74	$151.05
Nonpoverty areas, Cleveland	12,436,741	18	24.10
Suburbs	5,500,566	8	6.04
Total	68,071,891	100	38.70

[a]Analysis is limited to those agencies maintaining statistics by census tract. See Table Q.5b for list of agencies included.

SOURCE: Research Department, Welfare Federation of Cleveland.

Table Q.5a. Distribution of Clients Served by Voluntary and Public Welfare Agencies, by Function and Area, 1966[a]

TYPE OF AGENCY, FUNCTION, AND AREA	CLIENTS SERVED		EXPENDITURES		
	NUMBER	PER CENT	TOTAL	PER CENT	PER CAPITA CLIENTS SERVED
COUNSELING					
Voluntary—Red Feather					
Poverty area, Cleveland	2,511	22	$ 570,353	18	$223.58
Nonpoverty area, Cleveland	3,548	31	957,136	31	269.77
Suburbs	5,335	47	1,590,468	51	298.12
Total	11,394	100	3,117,957	100	273.65
Voluntary—Other					
Poverty area, Cleveland	1,513	31	223,990	19	148.04
Nonpoverty area, Cleveland	1,437	29	275,315	24	191.59
Suburbs	1,995	40	663,638	57	332.65
Total	4,945	100	1,162,943	100	235.18
Public	—	—	—	—	—
FAMILY SUPPORT AND EDUCATION					
Voluntary—Red Feather					
Poverty area, Cleveland	2,636	50	216,880	44	82.28
Nonpoverty area, Cleveland	1,641	31	118,014	24	71.92
Suburbs	1,020	19	162,894	32	159.70
Total	5,297	100	497,788	100	93.98
Voluntary—Other	—	—	—	—	—
Public					
Poverty area, Cleveland	36,969	63	49,333,597	74	1,334.46
Nonpoverty area, Cleveland	12,108	21	12,141,751	18	1,002.79
Suburbs	9,681	16	5,391,636	8	556.93
Total	58,758	100	66,866,984	100	1,138.01
GROUP SERVICES, LOCAL					
Voluntary—Red Feather					
Poverty area, Cleveland	17,481	53	1,255,232	44	71.81
Nonpoverty area, Cleveland	5,819	18	466,022	17	80.07
Suburbs	9,427	29	1,102,488	39	116.95
Total	32,727	100	2,823,742	100	86.28
Voluntary—Other	—	—	—	—	—
Public	—	—	—	—	—
GROUP SERVICES, NATIONAL					
Voluntary—Red Feather					
Poverty area, Cleveland	20,620	12	590,763	11	28.65
Nonpoverty area, Cleveland	33,883	20	1,007,093	19	29.72
Suburbs	117,752	68	3,819,410	70	32.44
Total	172,255	100	5,417,266	100	31.45
Voluntary—Other	—	—	—	—	—
Public	—	—	—	—	—

Table Q.5a (con't)

TYPE OF AGENCY, FUNCTION, AND AREA	CLIENTS SERVED		EXPENDITURES		
	NUMBER	PER CENT	TOTAL	PER CENT	PER CAPITA CLIENTS SERVED
HEALTH AND REHABILITATION					
Voluntary—Red Feather					
Poverty area, Cleveland	6,256	46	1,221,801	45	195.30
Nonpoverty area, Cleveland	3,294	24	699,804	26	212.45
Suburbs	4,107	30	766,169	29	186.55
Total	13,657	100	2,687,774	100	196.81
Voluntary—Other	—	—	—	—	—
Public	—	—	—	—	—
RESIDENTIAL CARE					
Voluntary—Red Feather					
Poverty area, Cleveland	261	23	842,381	22	3,227.51
Nonpoverty area, Cleveland	356	31	1,136,051	30	3,191.15
Suburbs	530	46	1,861,289	48	3,511.87
Total	1,147	100	3,839,721	100	3,347.62
Voluntary—Other					
Poverty area, Cleveland	23	29	226,788	29	9,860.35
Nonpoverty area, Cleveland	24	30	227,813	29	9,492.21
Suburbs	33	41	333,050	42	10,092.42
Total	80	100	787,651	100	9,845.64
Public					
Poverty area, Cleveland	552	65	800,987	67	1,451.06
Nonpoverty area, Cleveland	213	25	294,990	24	1,384.93
Suburbs	84	10	108,930	9	1,296.79
Total	849	100	1,204,907	100	1,419.21

[a]Analysis limited to those agencies maintaining statistics by census tract. See Table Q.5b for list of agencies included.
SOURCE: Research Department, Welfare Federation of Cleveland.

Table Q.5b. Agencies Included in Voluntary and Public Welfare Services, by Function

COUNSELING

Voluntary—Red Feather
  Catholic Counseling Center
  Children's Services
  Cleveland Guidance Center
  Family Service Association
  Jewish Children's Bureau
  Jewish Family Service Association
  Lutheran Children's Aid Society
  Nationalities Services Center
  Travelers Aid Society
  Youth Service

Voluntary—Other
  American Red Cross, Greater Cleveland Chapter
  Benjamin Rose Institute

Public
  None

FAMILY SUPPORT AND EDUCATION

Voluntary—Red Feather
  Day Nursery Association
  Euclid Day Care Center
  Legal Aid Society

Voluntary—Other
  None

Public
  Aid for Aged
  Aid to Blind
  Aid to Dependent Children
  Aid to Dependent Children of the Unemployed
  Aid to Permanently and Totally Disabled
  Division of Child Welfare
  General Relief
  Juvenile Court

GROUP SERVICES, LOCAL

Voluntary—Red Feather
  Cleveland Music School Settlement
  Garden Valley Neighborhood House
  Greater Cleveland Neighborhood Centers Association
  Jewish Community Center of Cleveland
  Karamu House
  Phillis Wheatley Association
  Urban League of Cleveland

Voluntary—Other
  None

Public
  None

Table Q.5b. (con't)

GROUP SERVICES, NATIONAL

Voluntary—Red Feather
  Boys Club of Cleveland
  Boy Scouts of America, Greater Cleveland Council
  Cleveland Council of Camp Fire Girls
  Lake Erie Girl Scout Council, Cleveland
  Young Men's Christian Association
  Young Women's Christian Association

Voluntary—Other
  None

Public
  None

HEALTH AND REHABILITATION

Voluntary—Red Feather
  Cleveland Hearing and Speech Center
  Cleveland Society for the Blind
  Goodwill Industries
  United Cerebral Palsy Association, Inc., of Cuyahoga County
  Visiting Nurse Association
  Vocational Guidance and Rehabilitation Services

Voluntary—Other
  None

Public
  None

RESIDENTIAL CARE

Voluntary—Red Feather
  Bellefaire Residential Treatment and Child Care Center
  Booth Memorial Hospital
  Catherina Horstmann Hospital
  Children's Aid Society
  DePaul Maternity and Infant Home
  Florence Crittenton Home
  Jewish Orthodox Home for Aged
  Marycrest School for Girls
  Parmadale
  Rose-Mary Johanna Grasselli Rehabilitation and Education Center
  St. Anthony Home for Boys

Voluntary—Other
  Beechbrook, Cleveland Protestant Children's Home
  Cleveland Christian Home
  Methodist Children's Home

Public
  Blossom Hill School
  Cleveland Boys' School
  Guild House—Division of Child Welfare

APPENDIX R
SOCIAL PROBLEM INDEX

Table R.1. Social Problem Index, by Selected Social Planning Areas[a]

	CENTRAL		EAST CENTRAL		WEST CENTRAL		DOWNTOWN		GLENVILLE		GOODRICH	
	RATE	RANK	RATE	RANK	RATE	RANK	RATE	RANK	RATE	RANK	RATE	RANK
Juvenile delinquency (male)	194.3	1	131.6	4	131.2	5	66.7	17	117.1	6	114.7	7
Child neglect and dependency	89.6	4	100.9	2	111.6	1	38.3	13	72.1	6	60.9	9
Private agency child placing	5.4	42	17.6	38	173.7	2	651.3	1	23.2	35	26.1	31
Illegitimate births	41.9	1	34.4	3	31.3	5	33.3	4	26.8	6	8.6	11
Aid for aged	445.6	2	296.8	5	492.8	1	405.1	3	218.8	7	142.2	8
General relief	125.9	3	65.7	6	129.4	2	462.2	1	46.3	7	36.2	8
Aid to dependent children	165.4	2	114.6	6	159.3	3	14.6	18	132.3	4	34.8	11
Tuberculosis, new cases	14.3	4	14.4	3	13.8	5	42.5	1	9.1	10	18.6	2
Infant mortality	3.3	5	2.7	12	4.0	2	—	28	3.4	4	3.0	7

	NORTH BROADWAY		TREMONT		HOUGH		KINSMAN		NEAR WEST SIDE	
	RATE	RANK	RATE	RANK	RATE	RANK	RATE	RANK	RATE	RANK
Juvenile delinquency (male)	75.7	14	100.9	9	155.6	2	112.3	8	91.1	10
Child neglect and dependency	43.0	12	55.4	10	78.0	5	95.0	3	45.8	11
Private agency child placing	68.8	5	35.5	20	16.2	39	9.6	41	129.0	4
Illegitimate births	8.3	12	7.9	13	35.8	2	25.8	7	7.3	14
Aid for aged	62.3	14	127.7	11	332.1	4	221.6	6	134.8	9
General relief	17.5	13	34.6	10	88.7	4	74.8	5	35.1	9
Aid to dependent children	24.3	13	55.9	8	205.5	1	130.6	5	37.7	10
Tuberculosis, new cases	7.2	12	11.0	6	9.3	9	10.3	7	9.4	8
Infant mortality	2.8	10	4.2	1	3.9	3	2.8	9	2.0	21

ᵃFor the purposes of this table, rate and rank are defined as follows.

Rate:
Juvenile Delinquency: Complaints filed in 1965 per 1,000, ages 12–17.
Child Neglect: Complaints filed in 1965 per 1,000 under 18 years.
Private Agency Child Placing: Accepted for continuing service by four agencies in 1965, per 10,000 under 18 years.
Illegitimate Births: Number per 100 total live births.
Aid for Aged: Number of recipients per 1,000 persons over 65 years.
General Relief: Number of recipients per 1,000 occupied family units.
Aid to Dependent Children: Recipients per 1,000 occupied family units.
Tuberculosis: Cases per 10,000 population.
Infant Mortality: Number of infant deaths per 100 live births.

Rank:
The areas are ranked to show comparative need as measured by each factor. The range is from greatest need (1) to least need (28) for Illegitimate Births and Infant Mortality; 42 social planning areas are used for all other factors.

SOURCE: Research Department, Welfare Federation of Cleveland, February, 1967; U.S. Census of Population, U.S. Bureau of the Census, 1965.

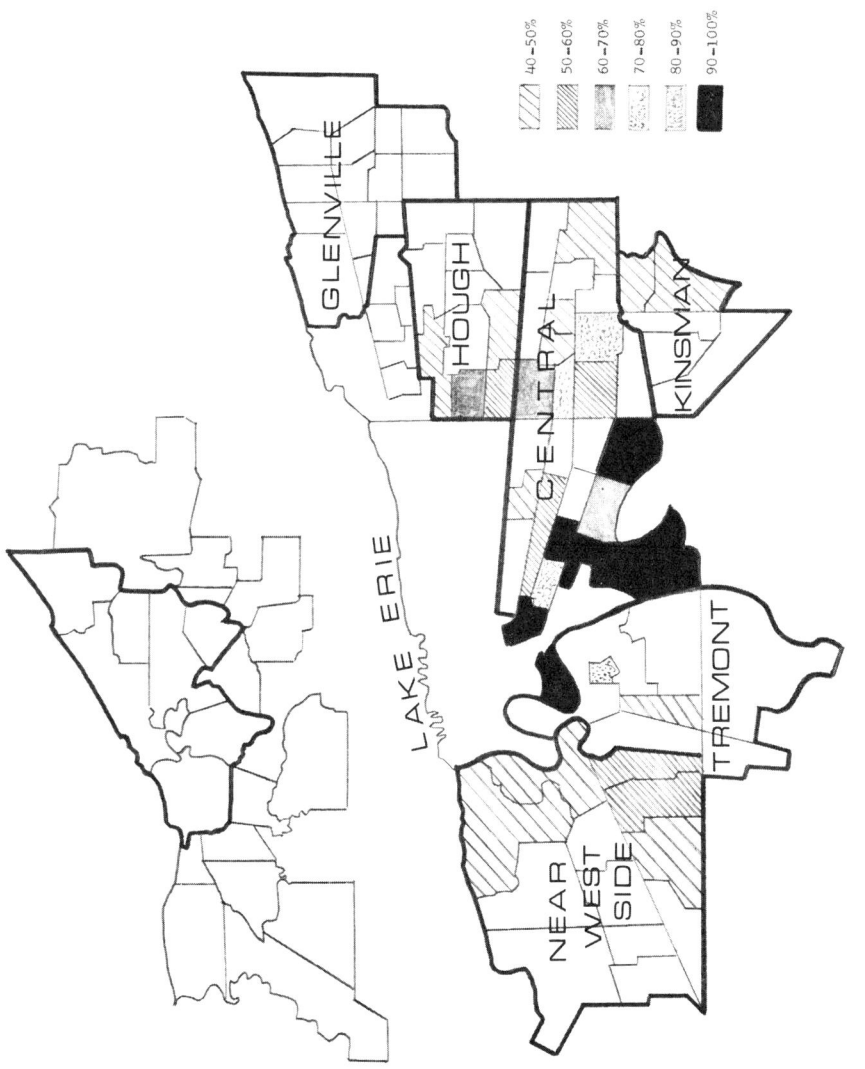

APPENDIX T
AREAS OF UNDEREMPLOYMENT OR UNEMPLOYMENT, CITY OF CLEVELAND, 1967*

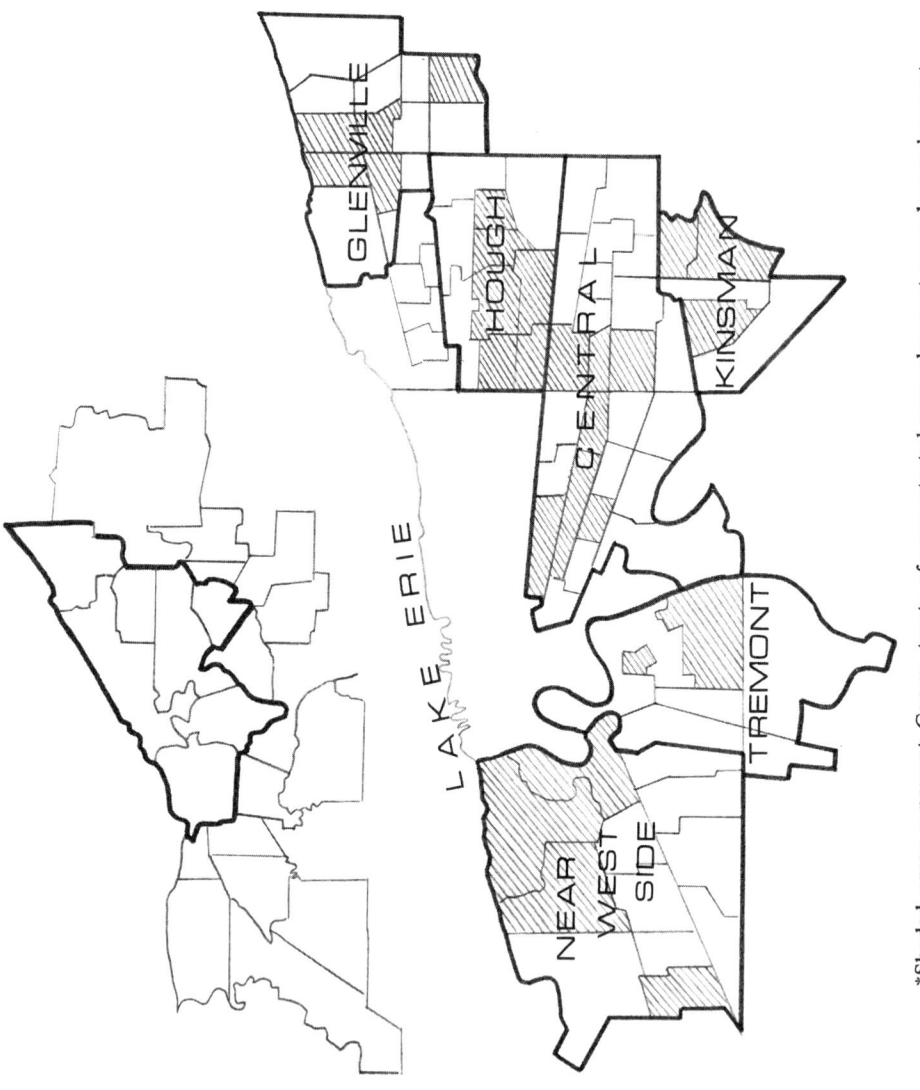

*Shaded areas represent Census tracts of concentrated unemployment or underemployment. Drawn from a listing provided by the U.S. Department of Labor, Manpower Administration, December, 1967.

SELECTED BIBLIOGRAPHY

Books

Burns, Eveline M., editor. *Children's Allowances and the Economic Welfare of Children,* The Report of a Conference. New York: Citizens' Committee for Children of New York, Inc., 1968.

Children in Need: A Study of a Federally Assisted Program of Aid to Needy Families with Children in Cleveland and Cuyahoga County, Ohio. Washington, D.C.: U. S. Commission on Civil Rights, 1966.

Elman, Richard M. *The Poorhouse State: The American Way of Life on Public Assistance.* New York: Pantheon Books, 1966.

Having the Power, We Have the Duty, Report of the Advisory Council on Public Welfare. Washington, D.C.: U. S. Government Printing Office, 1966.

Steiner, Gilbert Yale. *Social Insecurity: The Politics of Welfare.* Chicago: Rand McNally, 1966.

Theobald, Robert, editor. *The Guaranteed Income.* Garden City, N.Y.: Doubleday and Co., 1966.

Titmuss, Richard M. *Commitment to Welfare.* New York: Pantheon Books, 1968.

Journals

Health, Education, and Welfare INDICATORS.
Ohio Public Assistance Expenditures.
Ohio Public Welfare Statistics.
Poverty and Human Resources Abstracts.
Public Welfare.
Social Security Bulletin.
Welfare in Review.